KISSING SID JAMES

KISSING SID JAMES

by Robert Farquhar

JOSEF WEINBERGER PLAYS

LONDON

ESSEX COUNTY LIBRARY

First published in 2003
by Josef Weinberger Ltd
12-14 Mortimer Street, London, W1T 3JJ

Copyright © 2003 by Robert Farquhar
Copyright © 1993 as an unpublished dramatic composition by Robert Farquhar

The author has asserted his moral right to be identified as the author of the work in accordance with sections 77 and 78 of the Copyright Designs and Patents Act 1988.

ISBN 0 85676 266 0

This play is protected by Copyright. According to Copyright Law, no public performance or reading of a protected play or part of that play may be given without prior authorisation from Josef Weinberger Plays, as agent for the Copyright Owners.

From time to time it is necessary to restrict or even withdraw the rights of certain plays. **It is therefore essential to check with us before making a commitment to produce a play.**

NO PERFORMANCE MAY BE GIVEN WITHOUT A LICENCE

AMATEUR PRODUCTIONS
Royalties are due at least one calendar month prior to the first performance. A royalty quotation will be issued upon receipt of the following details:

Name of Licensee
Play Title
Place of Performance
Dates and Number of Performances
Audience Capacity
Ticket Prices

PROFESSIONAL PRODUCTIONS
All enquiries regarding professional rights (excluding first class rights) should be addressed to Josef Weinberger Plays at the above address. All other enquiries should be addressed to the Rod Hall Agency Ltd, 3 Charlotte Mews, London W1T 4DZ.

OVERSEAS PRODUCTIONS
Applications for productions overseas should be addressed to our local authorised agents. Further details are listed in our catalogue of plays, published every two years, or available from Josef Weinberger Plays at the address above.

CONDITIONS OF SALE
This book is sold subject to the condition that it shall not by way of trade or otherwise be resold, hired out, circulated or distributed without prior consent of the Publisher. **Reproduction of the text either in whole or part and by any means is strictly forbidden.**

Printed by Watkiss Studios Ltd, Biggleswade, Beds, England

For Charles and Terri

KISSING SID JAMES was first performed at the Unity Theatre, Liverpool on September 4th 1993, with the following cast:

EDDIE   Charles Bartholomew

CRYSTAL   Terri Morgan

Directed by Robert Farquhar

The play was subsequently performed by the Coliseum Theatre, Oldham in March 1995 and Hull Truck Theatre Company in the spring of 1999.

KISSING SID JAMES was co-produced by the Octagon Theatre, Bolton and Richard Jordan Productions Ltd and played at the Octagon Theatre from March 29th 2001, with the following cast:

EDDIE   Mark Chatterton

CRYSTAL   Teresa Gallagher

Directed by Mark Babych
Designed by Richard Foxton
Lighting and Sound design by Tom Weir

ACT ONE

Scene One

Light up on EDDIE. *He is nervously preparing himself to make a phone call. He eventually manages to press all the required digits. A phone rings. Light up on* CRYSTAL'S *phone. She enters. She is getting ready to go out.* EDDIE *hangs up though before she gets to it. She looks mystified.* EDDIE *tries again. He is breathing heavily.* CRYSTAL'S *phone rings. He waits. She picks it up.*

CRYSTAL	Hello. Crystal speaking.
	(EDDIE *cannot speak due to nerves.*)
CRYSTAL	Hello?
	(EDDIE *attempts to say something.*)
CRYSTAL	Look is this one of those phone calls?
EDDIE	No, no, no, Crystal, it's me.
CRYSTAL	Who?
EDDIE	Me. Eddie. Eddie. With the tash.
CRYSTAL	Oh. Eddie.
EDDIE	Yea, it's me. Eddie. So. The, er, yea, I was just, I expect you're thinking, the thing is I was just passing the phone, as you do, and I thought I shall give Crystal a bell, see how she is.
CRYSTAL	I'm just off out to work, Eddie.
EDDIE	Of course. Don't let me stop you. You're a busy woman. Things to do, all that, I've been very busy myself today. We are both very busy people. So, look . . .

CRYSTAL   At what, Eddie?

EDDIE   Oh yea, nice one. At what? Very good. Very quick off the mark, I like that. Anyway, look, I'll come straight to the point.

(*Pause.*)

CRYSTAL   Which is?

EDDIE   I am really sorry about the other night.

CRYSTAL   The other night?

EDDIE   In the Indian. You know, the bill and all that. I mean, those cards, they are normally legit anywhere you care to mention. I have dined out in some cracking places with that card. Cracking. They say thank you very much, that will do nicely sir. No bother. No hassle. One swipe and you can stuff your face. Normally. That waiter, eh, what charm school did he go to? I mean, I was shocked, Crystal, you could have knocked me down with a –

CRYSTAL   It's OK, Eddie, I'll forgive you.

EDDIE   Hey, it was just lucky you had your wages on you.

CRYSTAL   Yes.

EDDIE   It was an unfortunate freak event.

CRYSTAL   Yes, you said.

EDDIE   I cannot apologise enough.

CRYSTAL   Yea, you said that as well.

EDDIE   So. Look. Are you, are you off out somewhere?

CRYSTAL   I'm just off out to work, Eddie.

EDDIE	Of course, of course. You said. Work. Right. Hey, you have a good one.
CRYSTAL	I think that's my taxi.

(CRYSTAL *pays very little attention to what* EDDIE *is saying during the following speech. maybe even putting the phone down at one point.*)

EDDIE	Yea, I'll er I'll just probably, you know, I'll just probably play it by ear myself tonight. Watch a video. Early night for a change. Yea. Can't party every night can you? Up to Carlisle tomorrow. Not actually Carlisle, somewhere nearby that nobody's ever heard of, but, anyway, yea, stay in, that's the name of the game. Relax. Unwind. Stay in. Did you hear that fellar on the radio saying that staying in was the new going out?
CRYSTAL	It's been great chatting Eddie, but I really have to get off.
EDDIE	Crystal . . .
CRYSTAL	What is it, Eddie?

(*Pause.*)

EDDIE	Have I said, I am really sorry about the other night.
CRYSTAL	Eddie, look, my taxi, it's waiting. (*Off.*) OK, won't be a minute.
EDDIE	Crystal . . .
CRYSTAL	What?
EDDIE	What would you say if I were to say to you, if, it's just an idea, that's all it is, if I were to say, if I said, obviously I'm not saying, it's an idea, just, just put it on the, the, run it past you, as it were, so, yea, as I was saying, anyway, what if,

what about, oh God can I start again, I've lost my thread?

CRYSTAL   What do you want Eddie?

EDDIE   Weekend.

CRYSTAL   Eh?

EDDIE   This weekend.

CRYSTAL   This weekend?

EDDIE   Yes.

CRYSTAL   What about it?

EDDIE   Exactly.

CRYSTAL   Exactly what?

EDDIE   This weekend.

CRYSTAL   What are you flipping going on about, Eddie?

EDDIE   Us.

CRYSTAL   Us?

EDDIE   Yea. You. Me. This weekend?

          (*Beat.*)

EDDIE   It's on me.

          (*Beat.*)

CRYSTAL   It's on you?

EDDIE   Everything. What about it?

CRYSTAL   This weekend?

EDDIE   That's the one.

CRYSTAL   Me and you?

EDDIE	Us.
CRYSTAL	Where?
EDDIE	Somewhere . . . somewhere secluded.
CRYSTAL	Secluded?
EDDIE	Exclusive.
CRYSTAL	Exclusive?
EDDIE	Very.
CRYSTAL	Room service?
EDDIE	Oh, most definitely.
CRYSTAL	And we'd be alone?
	(*Beat.*)
EDDIE	If you want.
	(*Beat.*)
CRYSTAL	You and me, go away together, somewhere that's secluded, exclusive, room service, this weekend, all weekend, nobody else, just me and you, this weekend?
	(*Beat.*)
EDDIE	Crystal, I thought you'd never ask. I'll pick you up six o'clock Friday.
	(*Both look to audience. Lights snap to black.*)

Scene Two

Hotel bedroom. EDDIE *and* CRYSTAL *can be heard off-stage laughing and joking.*

CRYSTAL You are a case, Eddie. Mr and Mrs Smith.

EDDIE Very respectable name, Smith.

CRYSTAL I know but he didn't believe you. What are you doing?

EDDIE This key won't work.

CRYSTAL Twiddle it.

EDDIE I am twiddling it.

CRYSTAL Here, let me twiddle it.

EDDIE Aha. There we are.

(*The door opens.*)

EDDIE Shut your eyes.

CRYSTAL Why? What are you going to do?

EDDIE Go on, shut them.

CRYSTAL This is most unusual, Edward.

(EDDIE *guides* CRYSTAL *into room. She is enjoying herself.*)

EDDIE Hey, keep them shut.

CRYSTAL Eh, what are you up to? You're not going to do anything naughty, are you?

EDDIE Coming through!

CRYSTAL Oh, this had better be good, Eddie.

EDDIE OK. Open sesame.

(CRYSTAL *opens her eyes with great expectations. The room does not live up to them.*)

EDDIE	What do you think, eh? What do you reckon?
CRYSTAL	It's a bit . . . busy.
EDDIE	Eh? Busy?
CRYSTAL	And frilly. I've never been too keen on frilly.
EDDIE	That's probably just the lighting. You get the right lighting and it makes all the difference.
	(*Beat.*)
EDDIE	Hey let's get sorted out here, so, I'll put my stuff over here, there we are, and I shall put your, er, your . . .
CRYSTAL	Overnight valise.
EDDIE	I shall put your overnight valise just, here.
	(EDDIE *is scootering around the room nervously.*)
EDDIE	Hey, look at this.
CRYSTAL	What's that?
EDDIE	We have got all the business here. Tea. Coffee. Even got a couple of those herbal jobs. Lemon verbena. Oh, and, wait for it . . . instant cappuccino.
CRYSTAL	I can't stand those smelly teas.
EDDIE	I know exactly what you're saying there, Crystal. Sumo wrestler's jockstrap or what, eh? But at least they're there. At least we have the choice. They may not be to our personal taste but because you've laid out that extra bit more money –
CRYSTAL	I can see your car.

EDDIE	Eh?
CRYSTAL	There it is.

(EDDIE *joins* CRYSTAL *at window.*)

EDDIE	Looks good, doesn't it?
CRYSTAL	It's a lovely colour.
EDDIE	Dynamite orange.
CRYSTAL	It was very comfortable.
EDDIE	Power-assisted steering. Supple suspension pads. Reinforced foam seating, front and back. One hundred and sixty degree recline angle. Very generous leg-room. Stylish state-of-the-art dashboard. Surroundsound stereo.
CRYSTAL	What's that funny smell?
EDDIE	Smell?

(EDDIE *seeks the smell.*)

EDDIE	That's the sea-air, that is. Marvellous. Oh yes, I wouldn't mind being able to bottle that up and sell it.
CRYSTAL	Sea-air?
EDDIE	Yea. You city people you're not used to these natural aromas.
CRYSTAL	And where is the sea?
EDDIE	It's over there. Look.
CRYSTAL	Where?
EDDIE	There.

CRYSTAL	I can't see it.
EDDIE	Look follow my finger.
	(*Beat.*)
EDDIE	Got it?
CRYSTAL	That's the sea.
EDDIE	We'll go for a walk down there tomorrow.
	(*Beat.*)
CRYSTAL	It's dead quiet.
EDDIE	Off-season.
CRYSTAL	It's the middle of September.
EDDIE	All the kids are back at school. Makes all the difference.
CRYSTAL	I'm not too keen on quiet. It makes me feel a bit edgy.
EDDIE	Edgy? You?
CRYSTAL	Yea, I like a bit of noise. A bit of something happening.
EDDIE	Do you know Crystal, I never had you down as the edgy type? First time I saw you in the casino I thought there is a woman who is on top of herself. Very classy. In control. The way you called out the numbers, and the way you used that little stick. Oh yes, I was very impressed, Crystal.
CRYSTAL	You lost quite a bit of money that night, didn't you?
EDDIE	Swings and roundabouts, Crystal. Swings and roundabouts.

CRYSTAL   You were very reckless.

EDDIE   That's the way it goes. C'est la vie.

CRYSTAL   I remember thinking he doesn't know what he's doing.

EDDIE   I was merry, Crystal. I was celebrating. I had just clinched a very big deal concerning a rather large number of filing cabinets and a Japanese car factory in Sunderland.

CRYSTAL   Filing cabinets?

EDDIE   Remote control filing cabinets.

CRYSTAL   Remote control?

EDDIE   You can be sitting in your swivel chair, you're busy doing something else, you press the remote control and the drawer you require opens immediately.

CRYSTAL   And how do you get the file out?

EDDIE   Well, you get your secretary to do that.

CRYSTAL   Why couldn't she have opened the drawer in the first place?

(*Beat.*)

EDDIE   Hey, why don't we have some champagne?

CRYSTAL   Oh, Eddie. Can you afford it?

EDDIE   Afford it? Afford it? I'll have you know you are talking to one of the top stationery sales executives this side of the English Channel. Just you wait right there and I will order us up a bottle of the very best house champagne.

(EDDIE *saunters cockily over to the phone.*)

EDDIE Red or white?

CRYSTAL Eh?

EDDIE Red or white?

CRYSTAL Er, just champagne. Champagne colour.

EDDIE Oh yea. Right. Just joking.

(*He dials room service.*)

EDDIE Afford it? She said can you afford it? Ah, hello. Is that room service? Very good. Now, what I would like, as quick as humanly possible, is for you to get me . . . What? Oh yes, of course. Thirteen. Room thir-teen. OK mate, you write it down. I understand. If that's what they say you have to do, you must certainly do as they say so. (*To* CRYSTAL.) He's got to write it down. Apparently the management are sticklers for paperwork. Oh hello mate, found your biro have you? OK then. Room thirteen, that's me. Now what I would like is . . . what? Well, just scribble it a bit mate, get the circulation going. OK? How's that? OK then. Are we ready? No, thirteen mate, not thirty. Alright mate, simple mistake. Anyone could have done it. So, would it please be possible . . . Tipex? What do you want tipex for? Eh? Can't you just put a line through it? Well do you know where it is? No mate, I cannot ring back, I am desperate for champagne. One bottle of if you would be so kind. Yes, I am a bit annoyed, mate, seeing as you asked. I know, I know it's just the system, but from my point of view . . . what? I know, I know mate, you're only doing your job, exactly, so, what? Yes, I understand, it can get very lonely, I know . . . what? What? What?

(*Beat.*)

EDDIE	Well when did she walk out on you? Oh, I bet she didn't mean it. No, of course not. They say things like that don't they? Look mate, just get on the phone to her. Just say what you've said to me. Go on do it. No, now mate. Go for it. She will mate. What have you got to lose? Well, apart from that. Exactly. Go for it. Now. Yes. That's it. OK mate, it's nothing. Hold on, hold on, before you do that, can I have a bottle of champagne. Yes, I thought you had. Two glasses. Nicely chilled. Room thirteen. OK mate. Think nothing of it. My pleasure. Don't forget the champagne now. Look after yourself. I will. See you. As quick as poss. Bye mate. OK. I'll be seeing you. Bye.

(EDDIE *puts phone down.*)

EDDIE	Sorted. Champagne is on its way.

(*During the phone call* CRYSTAL *has disappeared into the bathroom.*)

EDDIE	Crystal?
CRYSTAL	(*off*) I'm in here.
EDDIE	Oh. Right. You're, you're in there. What's it like?
CRYSTAL	What's that?
EDDIE	The bathroom. What's it like?
CRYSTAL	It's very blue.
EDDIE	What? Tiles?
CRYSTAL	No, wallpaper.
EDDIE	Oh, blue wallpaper. Very tasteful. Is there a motif?
CRYSTAL	A what?

EDDIE   A motif? Does the wallpaper have a motif?

CRYSTAL   There's flowers all over it.

EDDIE   Flowers? Very good for bathrooms, flowers.
           My Mum's got flowers in her bathroom.
           They're plastic mind, but still, very serene. But
           you want that in a bathroom, don't you?

CRYSTAL   What?

EDDIE   Serenity? A bit of peace and quiet.

           (CRYSTAL *has emerged unnoticed by* EDDIE. *He
           is slightly shouting. A moment of
           awkwardness.*)

CRYSTAL   I was just putting my toothbrush out.

EDDIE   What a good idea. I must follow suit.

           (EDDIE *goes to suitcase and gets out his
           toiletries bag.*)

EDDIE   Here we are.

           (*Beat.*)

EDDIE   It's all in here.

CRYSTAL   Is it?

EDDIE   This bag has been quite a few places, I can tell
           you.

CRYSTAL   I'm sure it has.

EDDIE   Stayed overnight in Walsall just the other
           week.

CRYSTAL   What? In Poland?

EDDIE   No, no, Walsall, just outside Birmingham.

(Beat.)

EDDIE Right then, I'll just, go and . . . don't want it hanging over me.

CRYSTAL OK.

EDDIE Get it out of the way.

CRYSTAL Very sensible.

EDDIE Have you brought any toothpaste?

CRYSTAL Yes.

EDDIE Oh, right. Because I was simply thinking there, off the top of my head, I was thinking that maybe, if you had forgotten, it's easily done, you could use mine. It's one of them power tubes. Extra stripes. Apparently.

(Beat. Sexual tension.)

CRYSTAL I'll think about it.

EDDIE OK. No rush. Just thought I'd mention it. So, I'll, just . . .

(EDDIE *somehow manages to sidle into the bathroom without touching* CRYSTAL.)

EDDIE *(off)* Oh yes very tasteful. Smashing taps.

CRYSTAL What's that?

EDDIE Smashing taps. Very functional.

(EDDIE *re-enters.*)

EDDIE Hey, smashing toothbrush. Very classy.

CRYSTAL I like it.

EDDIE	I, I put my, toothbrush in the, the same glass, if that's alright?
CRYSTAL	That's perfectly OK, Eddie.
	(*Beat.*)
EDDIE	Are you OK? Everything to your requirements?
CRYSTAL	I'm fine Eddie. How are you?
EDDIE	Oh, I am great, me. Sailing. A-OK. No worries. Nope. No flies on Eddie baby.
CRYSTAL	You didn't have any doubts then?
EDDIE	Nah.
	(*Beat.*)
EDDIE	What sort of doubts?
CRYSTAL	You know, coming here.
EDDIE	Oh no, my mate Tezzer recommended it. He's very clued up on these sort of things is Tezzer. Because if there's one thing –
CRYSTAL	But . . .
EDDIE	What?
CRYSTAL	You didn't have any, little, niggling . . .
EDDIE	Eh?
CRYSTAL	You didn't think, just me and you, here. You didn't think . . .
EDDIE	What?
CRYSTAL	That we might not get on.
EDDIE	But we are getting on.

CRYSTAL	Yes, I know we are getting on ...
EDDIE	I've ordered the champagne. It's all sorted.
CRYSTAL	I've got to say Eddie, I was a bit worried ...
EDDIE	What about?
CRYSTAL	Us not getting on.
EDDIE	But we are getting on.
CRYSTAL	Yes, I know we are.
EDDIE	So what's the problem?
CRYSTAL	There isn't one.
EDDIE	Isn't there?
CRYSTAL	No. That's what I'm trying to say. I thought there might have been one but there isn't.
EDDIE	A problem?
CRYSTAL	No.
	(*Beat.*)
EDDIE	Smashing bathroom, though.
CRYSTAL	Oh yes, I'm a bathroom person, me. Nothing I like better than a steaming hot bath, a good book, and a facepack.
EDDIE	I had a jacuzzi put in our bath at home.
CRYSTAL	Oh, what's that like?
EDDIE	Well worth it. Not cheap but very well worth it. Very good for opening up the pores. Personal hygiene, mega-important, eh?

CRYSTAL	I like listening to music as well.
EDDIE	Oh yes. I'm all fixed up there. I've got speakers specially built in. I've got one of them Bang-Olfsen highfibre numbers. Matt black. Oh yes, music first thing in the morning. Gets you in the mood. Something slightly uptempo. Obviously not too uptempo, just a notch down from fully uptempo. Sort of midtempo. Midtempo with a bit more tempo than . . . normal midtempo.
	(*Beat.*)
CRYSTAL	Eddie?
EDDIE	What's that?
CRYSTAL	You said our bathroom?
EDDIE	No, I couldn't have said that.
CRYSTAL	You did.
EDDIE	Nah. Who'd live with me, eh? Hey, where is that champagne?
	(EDDIE *goes to door.*)
EDDIE	Nope. No sign.
	(*Beat.*)
EDDIE	Fancy a cup of tea? Before the champagne. Sort of aperitif?
CRYSTAL	No it's OK, Eddie.
EDDIE	Spot of telly?
CRYSTAL	No.
EDDIE	Yes, you take it easy. Make yourself at home. What's the time? Oh getting on.

CRYSTAL	Why don't you take your jacket off?
EDDIE	Eh?
	(*Beat.*)
EDDIE	Good idea. Relax. Unwind. Take it easy.
	(EDDIE *takes his jacket off and puts it over a chair.*)
CRYSTAL	What about music?
EDDIE	What about it?
CRYSTAL	Why don't we have some?
EDDIE	Good idea. That is a very very good idea.
	(EDDIE *goes to bedside radio.*)
EDDIE	Music, coming up. Hey haven't seen something like this for, oh must be since Tony Blackburn was doing the breakfast show. But they do the job. As we say. Okey-dokey, music, music, music, where be some music
	(EDDIE *tunes into 'Je t'aime'. He registers this, and then moves the dial on.*)
EDDIE	I'll just have a fiddle, see what else there is.
	(*A few snatches of what we soon realise is 'Sexual Healing' by Marvin Gaye.*)
CRYSTAL	That sounds alright.
EDDIE	I'll see what it sounds like on FM. Better reception.
	(*A Radio 4-type announcer.*)

MAN	And now on Radio Freehold a dramatisation of the life and times of Peter Stringfellow. Episode one, Casanova Comes of Age.
EDDIE	I don't think that's quite what we want.
CRYSTAL	Eddie, what about the first one?
EDDIE	No, no, here we are.
	(*A radio phone-in.*)
DOCTOR	And our next caller is John from Birmingham.
JOHN	Hello there doctor I'd like to talk to you about premature ejaculation.
	(EDDIE *quickly tries to retune.*)
CRYSTAL	Eddie . . .
EDDIE	It's OK, I know what I'm doing, as the man on the Titanic said . . .
	(*Back to 'Je t'aime'.*)
CRYSTAL	Eddie, leave it on that station.
EDDIE	OK, whatever you say. Sure thing. That's . . . fine with me.
	(*The music plays.*)
CRYSTAL	I've always wanted to learn French.
EDDIE	Hey there's a card in our local newsagents. I'll get you the number if you want.
CRYSTAL	I love the way they hold themselves. The French.
EDDIE	Oh yes, they're very good at that. That, and, and –

CRYSTAL	I love the way the men shrug their shoulders and dangle the cigarettes out of their mouths.
EDDIE	Oh yes, your average Brit, we couldn't manage that. It wouldn't look right would it? I mean, I'm very fond of the French. They are a bit arrogant, and garlic has never been a favourite, but they are smashing, wonderful people. I mean that fellar who did those hair adverts, I know some people say he doesn't pull his weight on the field, but –
CRYSTAL	Eddie.
EDDIE	Hello?
CRYSTAL	The lighting.
EDDIE	The lighting?
CRYSTAL	Do you think we could have it a bit dimmer?
EDDIE	A bit . . .
CRYSTAL	Dimmer.
EDDIE	A bit dimmer? I should think so. Certainement madamoselle. You want it dimmer it shall be dimmer. Oh yes. Now just you say when it's dim enough. OK?
CRYSTAL	OK.

(*The room snaps into black-out.*)

CRYSTAL	I think that's a bit too dim, Eddie.

(*Lights up.*)

EDDIE	Sorry about that, let's have another go. Sorry about this, it's got a bit jammed up here.
CRYSTAL	Eddie, if it's a problem . . .

EDDIE	No, here we are. Got the hang of it.
	(*Into darkness.*)
CRYSTAL	Eddie...
EDDIE	Got it sussed, normal service will be resumed as soon as possible. There we are.
	(EDDIE *starts playing madly with the lights.*)
CRYSTAL	Eddie, what are you doing?
EDDIE	I'm just loosening it up.
CRYSTAL	Eddie please, do you really have to do –
EDDIE	I'm just not used to the make. My dimmer at home is much more user friendly. I'm sure if I just play with it for a bit –
CRYSTAL	Eddie, just leave it –
EDDIE	I've started so I'll finish.
CRYSTAL	Eddie...
EDDIE	No need to panic...
CRYSTAL	Eddie, honestly, Eddie...
	(*Suddenly the room finds an atmospheric dimness.*)
EDDIE	There we are. Sorted.
	(*The music is still playing.* EDDIE *returns to the bed.*)
CRYSTAL	So. Eddie.
EDDIE	That's me.
CRYSTAL	Soft lighting. Sexy music.

EDDIE	He's dead now.
CRYSTAL	Who is?
EDDIE	The fellar on this record.
CRYSTAL	Is he?
EDDIE	Comes to us all.
CRYSTAL	What does?
EDDIE	Death.
CRYSTAL	I know it does.
EDDIE	Makes you think.
CRYSTAL	Eddie.
EDDIE	Apparently . . .
CRYSTAL	Shuush.
	(EDDIE *starts to articulate*.)
CRYSTAL	Ah.
	(*Silence.*)
EDDIE	Is this it?
CRYSTAL	This is it, Eddie.
	(*Fade to black. Music up.*)

Scene Three

The music continues. EDDIE *and* CRYSTAL *are now in bed. All of this scene is played in darkness, maybe some light from an outside street lamp. Fumblings, groans, etc.*

CRYSTAL	Eddie.
EDDIE	Crystal.
CRYSTAL	Eddie please.
EDDIE	Oh Crystal.
CRYSTAL	No Eddie.
EDDIE	Oh yes, Crystal.
CRYSTAL	No, Eddie, stop, stop it.
EDDIE	Eh?
CRYSTAL	Could you just, that's better . . .
EDDIE	What's up?
CRYSTAL	Look Eddie, don't you think you should put on a condom?
EDDIE	What? You mean . . .
CRYSTAL	A condom.
EDDIE	Yea, yea, I was thinking about that.
CRYSTAL	And?
EDDIE	It's a good idea. A very very good idea.
CRYSTAL	I know it's a good idea.
EDDIE	But . . .
CRYSTAL	What?
EDDIE	I haven't got any.
CRYSTAL	You haven't got any condoms?

EDDIE	Well, obviously I've got condoms, I've got stacks, well when I say, a few, you know, this day and age and all that, I've got a couple, but, it's just, you know how it is.
CRYSTAL	You haven't brought any with you, have you?
EDDIE	No.
CRYSTAL	Why not?
EDDIE	I didn't want to appear too forward.
CRYSTAL	Too forward? You asked me away for the weekend.
EDDIE	That is true, I did ask you away for the weekend. That is correct, and obviously I, I, it's just, I didn't want you to think I was only after you for one thing.
CRYSTAL	Charming, so you didn't want to sleep with me?
EDDIE	No no no no I, er, I wanted to respect you as a human being.
CRYSTAL	I do not believe this.
EDDIE	I'll phone room service.
CRYSTAL	No.
EDDIE	It's alright he knows me. He's my mate.
CRYSTAL	Eddie, you are not phoning room service.
EDDIE	Oh God, it's all going wrong.
CRYSTAL	Eddie. Calm down.
EDDIE	It's all my fault.
CRYSTAL	Eddie, please . . .

EDDIE	And it was all going so well.
CRYSTAL	Look, will you take this.
EDDIE	I know I know I know I should have brought some.
CRYSTAL	Eddie, Eddie, take this.
EDDIE	Eh? What's this?
CRYSTAL	It's an inflatable dinghy! What do you think it is?
EDDIE	It's a condom!
CRYSTAL	Yes.
EDDIE	Right. OK. Right. Enough said.

(*Beat.*)

EDDIE	Right then. Won't be a moment.
CRYSTAL	Would you like a hand?
EDDIE	Eh?
CRYSTAL	Let me help you.
EDDIE	It's man's work, this.
CRYSTAL	Eddie, will you just give it here.
EDDIE	I don't know what's what here.
CRYSTAL	Eddie, look . . .
EDDIE	What?
CRYSTAL	Will you just . . .
EDDIE	What?

CRYSTAL	Shut up for a moment.
	(*Activity under sheets.*)
CRYSTAL	Now...
	(*More activity.*)
EDDIE	I wonder how many people are doing this round the country at this very moment?
CRYSTAL	Eddie, would you just, keep still.
EDDIE	How would you do a survey for something like that? Ow!
CRYSTAL	I said keep still.
EDDIE	I did keep still.
CRYSTAL	Oh look, it's OK.
EDDIE	For crying out loud...
CRYSTAL	What's up now?
EDDIE	It's caught underneath.
CRYSTAL	It is not, don't overreact.
EDDIE	Hey how would you bloody like it?
CRYSTAL	For goodness sake Eddie...
EDDIE	Here you are, let me do it...
CRYSTAL	It's alright, I know what I'm doing.
EDDIE	Look, I can do it, no bother...
CRYSTAL	Eddie.
EDDIE	What?

CRYSTAL	This is supposed to be foreplay.
EDDIE	Is it?
CRYSTAL	Yes.
	(*Beat.*)
CRYSTAL	There we are.
	(CRYSTAL *lies back.* EDDIE *lies back as well.*)
EDDIE	Snug as a bug. You did a lovely job there Crystal.
	(*Beat.*)
EDDIE	Right then. Where were we?
CRYSTAL	Eddie.
EDDIE	What?
CRYSTAL	Could you not talk so much?
EDDIE	Eh?
CRYSTAL	Don't talk. I don't like it.
EDDIE	You don't like, talking?
CRYSTAL	No.
EDDIE	Not whilst we're . . .
CRYSTAL	No.
EDDIE	OK. Understood. No talking.
CRYSTAL	It's just, you know, I just prefer it if –
EDDIE	Your secret is safe with me.
CRYSTAL	What do you mean by that?

EDDIE   Eh?

CRYSTAL   Are you implying that I'm strange or something?

EDDIE   No, no, I was, just saying that your, your, secret will be safe with me.

CRYSTAL   It's not a secret.

EDDIE   I'm not saying it is.

CRYSTAL   Makes me sound like some sort of weirdo.

EDDIE   No, no what I meant was –

CRYSTAL   It's just I used to know someone who, who did it and, look, all I'm saying is that I'd prefer it if you didn't.

EDDIE   Say no more.

CRYSTAL   I don't mind if you moan.

EDDIE   Moaning. Can do.

CRYSTAL   Maybe some low whispering.

EDDIE   Rightio. Low whispering.

CRYSTAL   And you can say my name if you want.

EDDIE   Say your name every now and then. Low whispering. Moaning. Got it. Fantastic. No problem.

(*Beat. Nothing happens.*)

EDDIE   Fantastic.

(*Beat.*)

EDDIE   No problem.

	(*Beat.*)
EDDIE	Hey, I like that lamp shade.
CRYSTAL	Eddie.
	(*They start to fumble underneath the sheets. Potential for moanings, and all the attendant comedy of clumsy lovemaking. Things proceed, and begin to reach a certain pitch of excitement.* EDDIE *starts to mumble, quite faintly at first.*)
EDDIE	Right, Gary Sprake, and then there was Reaney, Paul Reaney, Paul Madeley, oh yes, Crystal, Billy Bremner...
CRYSTAL	Eddie!?
EDDIE	Billy Bremner, oh no, must, oh yes, Billy Bremner, and then, then, oh my...
CRYSTAL	Eddie, Eddie?!
EDDIE	Jackie Charlton, yes, and then the one who bit yer legs...
CRYSTAL	Eddie, stop this, now, Eddie!
EDDIE	Norman Hunter, Eddie Gray...
CRYSTAL	Eddie!!
	(*Silence.*)
EDDIE	What's up?
CRYSTAL	Stop it.
EDDIE	What?
CRYSTAL	Talking.

EDDIE   I wasn't, was I?

CRYSTAL   Ten to the flipping dozen. Who is Billy Bremner?

EDDIE   Billy Bremner?

CRYSTAL   Why are you going on about Billy Bremner?

EDDIE   He was the captain of the classic Leeds United team of the 1970s.

CRYSTAL   Well, what's he doing in this bed?

EDDIE   It's just a sort of method I have.

CRYSTAL   Method? I don't believe this.

EDDIE   It won't happen again.

           (*Beat.*)

EDDIE   Sorry.

CRYSTAL   I told you I don't like talking.

EDDIE   Say no more. No talking. Message received, fully comprehendez, I will not talk, at all, no, definitely not, not a syllable will pass my lips, no, no talking, shut up Eddie.

           (*Beat. They start to fumble again.* EDDIE *is all rush again, and soon things get very worked up, and again he starts to mumble.*)

EDDIE   Right, Gordon Banks, Ray Wilson, and the one you always forget . . .

CRYSTAL   Eddie?

EDDIE   Cohen, George Cohen, that's it, oh God, and –

CRYSTAL   Eddie.

EDDIE	And, Bobby Moore, oh yes, there was a footballer, and, and –
CRYSTAL	This isn't funny Eddie.
EDDIE	Jackie Charlton, he cropped up before didn't he? Oh God . . .
CRYSTAL	Stop it, Eddie.
EDDIE	Nobby Stiles, yes, yes, think of Nobby Stiles.
CRYSTAL	Move your leg.
EDDIE	Doing his little dance without his teeth in . . .
CRYSTAL	Eddie, will you . . . Eddie!
EDDIE	Oh yes, oh no, Martin Peters, Alan Ball, oh no, Geoff Hurst . . .
CRYSTAL	Eddie!
EDDIE	Oh . . . some people are on the pitch . . . they think it's all over.

(*Things come to a conclusion from* EDDIE'S *point of view.*)

EDDIE	It is now.

(*Silence.*)

CRYSTAL	Get off, Eddie.
EDDIE	Eh?
CRYSTAL	Get off. Now.
EDDIE	Give us a minute.
CRYSTAL	Move.

(EDDIE *moves. He is knackered.*)

EDDIE	Hey Crystal, did the earth move? Eh?
	(*Silence.*)
EDDIE	Crystal?
	(*Silence.*)
EDDIE	Only joking. Crystal?
	(*Silence. The sound of crashing waves.*)

Scene Four

On the beach. CRYSTAL *and* EDDIE *have gone for a walk.* EDDIE *has a pair of binoculars.*

EDDIE	Oh yes look at the wingspan on that. Marvellous. Hey, Crystal, would you care to admire the regal swoop of the majestic creature circling above our earthbound heads?
CRYSTAL	What are you on about?
EDDIE	The seagull. Do you want to have a look at the seagull?
CRYSTAL	I can see it from here.
EDDIE	I know, but you get a close-up with these.
CRYSTAL	I can live without it.
EDDIE	Hey, look what it's doing now. Mag-bloody-nificient. Oh nature, you can't beat it. It's the sort of thing that could make a grown man come over all poetic.
CRYSTAL	Is it?
EDDIE	Oh yes, this is the life. Morning.

CRYSTAL	Do you have to say good morning to every person who comes within a hundred yard radius?
EDDIE	Just being friendly.
CRYSTAL	You said good morning to him ten minutes ago.
EDDIE	They like you to be friendly up here.
CRYSTAL	They don't smile much.
EDDIE	Well, that's their nature. They don't smile much, but if you were in a spot of bother, they'd sell their great-Grandmother's zimmer frame. Morning. Smashing day, eh?
CRYSTAL	And Eddie it is not a smashing day, it's freezing.
EDDIE	It's not freezing, it's breezy.
CRYSTAL	Look at those clouds.
EDDIE	They'll pass.
CRYSTAL	What? They've been here since we got here.
EDDIE	Those clouds haven't.
CRYSTAL	They have.
EDDIE	To be precise, those clouds haven't. On a day like today, what with it being quite breezy, those clouds have not technically been there since we got here, because of course ten minutes ago they would –
CRYSTAL	Alright Eddie, I get the point.
	(*Silence.*)
EDDIE	Do you know I could stand here for hours just watching the waves.

CRYSTAL	Could you?
EDDIE	Oh yes. The ebb and flow of forces greater than yourself. Very humbling.

(*Silence.*)

CRYSTAL	Do you think that's seaweed?
EDDIE	Very nutritious, seaweed. Full of vitamins.
CRYSTAL	I always thought seaweed was green.
EDDIE	Will you get an eyeful of that?
CRYSTAL	What is it?
EDDIE	That's an eagle that is.
CRYSTAL	That's not an eagle.
EDDIE	It is. It's one of them sea-eagles. Morning! Did you see that eagle? Yea, a sea-eagle, I saw it on one of them nature programmes.
CRYSTAL	He doesn't believe you.
EDDIE	He does. You what mate? It's a what, no, you want to get your eyes tested. Eh? Alright, just joking, OK, OK, yea, same to you, mate.

(*Beat.*)

EDDIE	Obviously not a local.

(*Beat.*)

EDDIE	Do you know I wouldn't mind retiring somewhere like here? Find a nice little bungalow with a seaview. Get myself an Alsatian. Very clever dogs, Alsatians. The dolphins of the dog world. Take it for a walk down here every day. 'There you go boy,

	fetch'. Smashing. It is quiet. I'll give you that. But you don't want to retire somewhere noisy, do you? You want to take it easy. Mull over your memories. Watch the telly. Play all your old forty-fives from yesteryear. Wear your favourite v-neck jumper. Oh yes, I could see myself doing that. Get my commerative gold-plated timepiece and head for somewhere like here.
CRYSTAL	What do you want to retire to somewhere like here for? It's grey, dreary and horrible.
EDDIE	That's only a surface impression. I'm sure if you lived here for a bit . . .
CRYSTAL	I'd rather die than come and live here.
EDDIE	Yea, but I'm not talking about coming to live here, I'm talking about coming to retire here.
	(*Beat.*)
EDDIE	Hey let's go for a walk.
CRYSTAL	Isn't that what we've been doing?
EDDIE	Come on, apparently you get an unspoilt view of the chemical works if you keep going this way.
CRYSTAL	No Eddie.
EDDIE	It's not far. Half-an-hour at max.
CRYSTAL	Half-an-hour? Eddie, these shoes are made for busy High Streets with lots of people spending their money, doing normal things like that, not for tramping up and down some grubby beach up the back end of nowhere.
EDDIE	Look, we'll just go up to the end and back again. We might see some crabs if we're lucky.

CRYSTAL	Crabs?
EDDIE	Yea, come on. It'll be an adventure.
CRYSTAL	An adventure? Why didn't you tell me? I would have brought my torch.
EDDIE	Come on.
CRYSTAL	I am not going anywhere near where there might be crabs.
EDDIE	What is wrong with crabs?
CRYSTAL	I don't trust anything that moves sideways.
EDDIE	They're alright.
CRYSTAL	And those eyes on stalks, it's not natural. And it is going to rain.
EDDIE	It is not going to rain.
CRYSTAL	It is.
EDDIE	It isn't.

(*Silence.* EDDIE *decides to try and be romantic.*)

EDDIE	Hey Crystal.
CRYSTAL	What?
EDDIE	Let's go for a walk.
CRYSTAL	Eh?
EDDIE	The tide's going out.
CRYSTAL	Eddie.
EDDIE	That's my name.

CRYSTAL	Are you looking at me?
EDDIE	I might be.
CRYSTAL	But you're looking at me aren't you?
EDDIE	How do you mean?
CRYSTAL	Going all gooey.
EDDIE	Gooey? How do you go all gooey?
CRYSTAL	Next thing I know you'll be wanting us to hold hands and stroll off into the sunset.
	(*Beat.*)
EDDIE	I thought women liked that sort of thing.
CRYSTAL	I don't. Not at the moment.
	(*Beat.*)
EDDIE	It's a dying art anyway.
CRYSTAL	What is?
EDDIE	Romance. I blame the Royal Family.
CRYSTAL	Can we not just go and find somewhere to sit down?
EDDIE	We'll get a couple of deckchairs. There was the old boy back there with the nasty cough and the hankie on his head.
CRYSTAL	It is going to rain, Eddie.
EDDIE	It is not going to rain.
CRYSTAL	It is. Look at those clouds.
EDDIE	I am looking but no rain do I see.

CRYSTAL	I can smell it coming.
EDDIE	Smell it? Who do you think you are? Hiawatha?
CRYSTAL	It is going to rain, Eddie.
EDDIE	It is not going to rain.
CRYSTAL	It is.
EDDIE	It is not.
CRYSTAL	It is.
EDDIE	It is not.
CRYSTAL	It is.
EDDIE	It is not going to rain.

(*On cue, a thunderclap.* EDDIE *and* CRYSTAL *are caught frozen by a flash of lightning. They look up at the skies as the rain begins to fall.*)

Scene Five

The sound of heavy rainfall continues. Back in the bedroom. EDDIE *stands looking out of the window.* CRYSTAL *comes out of the bathroom with a towel round her head.*

EDDIE	Doesn't look like letting up much.
	(*Beat.*)
EDDIE	Looks like we're stuck here for a bit.
	(*Beat.*)
EDDIE	Still, the garden needs it. As my Mum always says.

(EDDIE *begins to wander round the room.*
CRYSTAL *has settled down, and fetched out a
big romantic novel.*)

EDDIE   What's that?

CRYSTAL   It's a book.

EDDIE   Oh, is it? Oh wow, a book. Hey look everyone, Crystal's reading a book.

CRYSTAL   Haven't you brought one?

EDDIE   I would have done, but you know how it is, I'm a big reader me, but, last minute top level meeting, that sort of thing,

(EDDIE *wanders round the room. he shouts at someone outside.*)

EDDIE   Will you look at that rain? Hey mate, it's raining. Raining. I said, yes, raining. You want to get yourself an umbrella.

(*Beat.*)

EDDIE   He wants to get himself an umbrella.

(*Beat.*)

EDDIE   Any good, is it?

CRYSTAL   Not bad.

EDDIE   Lot of pages.

CRYSTAL   Yes.

EDDIE   Would you mind, Crystal, if I just . . .

(EDDIE *steals* CRYSTAL'S *book.*)

CRYSTAL   Oh Eddie, what are you doing?

| EDDIE | I just want to see how many pages it's got. |

(EDDIE *checks this.*)

| EDDIE | Nine hundred and eighty-nine. |

(EDDIE *is impressed. He gives the book back*).

| EDDIE | My Mum likes to read. Mills and Boon. That sort of stuff. Nothing too racy. She's got hundreds. Hey, nine hundred and eighty-nine!? What page are you up to? |

(CRYSTAL *ignores* EDDIE.)

EDDIE	Crystal?
CRYSTAL	Seventy-three.
EDDIE	Seventy-three. Just started, eh? So, let's work that out, seventy-three, take that away from eight hundred, no nine hundred and, what was it again, look let's call it a thousand. So seventy-three, minus, what did I say, anyway, you've got quite a way to go there. That is a lot of pages. A lot of words. How many words to a page do you reckon?
CRYSTAL	Eddie, do you mind, this is a good bit.

(EDDIE *wanders. He fetches out a camera.*)

| EDDIE | Crystal? Smile! |

(CRYSTAL *does a false smile to camera.* EDDIE *takes the photograph.*)

EDDIE	I'll call that one study of Crystal with book. Hey, did it flash?
CRYSTAL	Yes.
EDDIE	Are you sure? I'm sure it didn't flash.

CRYSTAL	Eddie, it flashed.
	(EDDIE *is slightly chastised. He wanders round the room, taking the odd photograph of whatever takes his fancy. He wanders back to the window.*)
EDDIE	Oh. Oh, will you look at that . . .
	(CRYSTAL *does not react.*)
EDDIE	In this weather. Would you believe it?
	(*Beat.*)
EDDIE	Hey Crystal, there's a fellar with no clothes on running about down here.
CRYSTAL	Is there?
EDDIE	He looks a bit like one of them Chippendales actually. Hey and he's doing a cartwheel! Crystal. There is a man with no clothes on performing an elaborate physical manoeuvre right outside our window.
	(*Beat.*)
EDDIE	You didn't believe me, did you?
CRYSTAL	No.
	(EDDIE *wanders, playing with things. He finds a Bible in the drawer next to the bed.*)
EDDIE	What do we have here? Do you know I have never actually read this. Terrible to admit, but true. No time like the present though. Hello, what's this? The book of Genesis. Do you think that's where they got the name from?
CRYSTAL	I would have thought so.
EDDIE	You learn something new every day.

(EDDIE *reads.*)

EDDIE 'In the beginning God created the Heaven and the Earth . . .' Good beginning.

(EDDIE *soon gets bored, and starts flicking through the pages.*)

EDDIE Do you know where all that stuff about Sodom and Gomorrah is?

CRYSTAL Why don't you look it up in the index?

EDDIE Good idea. That is a very very good idea.

(EDDIE *looks for the index.*)

EDDIE Hey, there isn't one.

CRYSTAL Of course there isn't. It's the Bible.

EDDIE Why can't the Bible have an index?

CRYSTAL To be honest, Eddie, I have never given the matter much thought. Why don't you phone room service and ask him?

(*End of conversation.* CRYSTAL *reads.* EDDIE *puts down Bible. He starts reading over her shoulder.*)

CRYSTAL Don't do that, Eddie.

EDDIE Eh?

CRYSTAL Don't read over my shoulder.

(*Beat.*)

EDDIE You sounded like my Mum there.

CRYSTAL Did I?

EDDIE	'Don't do that'. She always says that.
CRYSTAL	You don't half talk about your Mum a lot.
EDDIE	No I don't.
CRYSTAL	Yes you do. She's forever cropping up.
EDDIE	Well, she's my Mum. People talk about their Mums.
CRYSTAL	Men do.
EDDIE	Women talk about their Mums, too.
CRYSTAL	Not like men. They're always dropping them into the conversation.
EDDIE	Well it's biological, isn't it?
	(*Silence.* EDDIE *goes back to reading over* CRYSTAL's *shoulder. It is obviously quite racy.*)
CRYSTAL	Eddie!
	(CRYSTAL *throws the book down in frustration.*)
CRYSTAL	For crying out loud, Eddie!
EDDIE	(*innocent*) What?
CRYSTAL	How can I read my book with you pacing about like this? You've got the concentration span of a goldfish.
EDDIE	Look, read your book. Just ignore me.
CRYSTAL	How can I ignore you in a room this size?
EDDIE	I'll sit still. Promise.
CRYSTAL	Forget it.
EDDIE	Look, I'm sitting still.

CRYSTAL	Forget it.
EDDIE	I won't budge. Look, I'm hardly breathing.
CRYSTAL	Forget it!

(*Silence.* CRYSTAL *now gets up and goes to the window.* EDDIE *is wary of what she will do next. She is thinking. He picks up the discarded book and starts to browse it. Eventually* CRYSTAL *speaks.*)

CRYSTAL	What's your sexual fantasy, Eddie?
EDDIE	Eh?
CRYSTAL	Your sexual fantasy. What is it?

(*Beat.*)

EDDIE	What you asking me that for?
CRYSTAL	I'm interested.
EDDIE	What, you mean . . .
CRYSTAL	Out of anyone in the world Eddie, who would you like to go to bed with?
EDDIE	Blimey. The entire world?
CRYSTAL	Yea. Think of all those women, Eddie.

(*Beat.*)

EDDIE	This is going back a few years, but I always used to think about Angela Rippon.
CRYSTAL	Angela Rippon?
EDDIE	When she showed her legs off that time on the *Morecambe and Wise Show*.

CRYSTAL	Come on, Eddie. Someone with a bit of you know what.
EDDIE	Right . . .
CRYSTAL	Someone with a bit of allure and oomph.
EDDIE	Oomph?
CRYSTAL	Yea.
EDDIE	Can I have a few minutes to think about it?

(CRYSTAL *is frustrated by* EDDIE'S *inability to play the game.*)

EDDIE	What about you then?
CRYSTAL	Sean Connery.
EDDIE	Sean Connery?
CRYSTAL	Sean Connery.
EDDIE	He's eligible for a bus pass.
CRYSTAL	So what?
EDDIE	That's disgusting.
CRYSTAL	You're just jealous.
EDDIE	Yea, I'm jealous of his money.
CRYSTAL	Oh yes, Sean Connery.
	(*Beat.*)
CRYSTAL	I'd be resting on my bed at home. And I'd have put on clean sheets and I'd have lit loads of candles and I'd have just had a nice long bath. And the pillows would be all puffed up, and I'd be waiting. I would be waiting in a state of complete and utter openness.

EDDIE That would be the bath, opens the pores.

CRYSTAL And I'd be wearing a pair of black stockings, and a flimsy see-thru nightie thing. And I'd be waiting, anticipating, and I'd be watching the telly, some sexy foreign thing. And then the door would slowly edge open, and this big male masculine shadow would just sort of emerge. And it would be him.

EDDIE Who?

CRYSTAL Sean.

EDDIE Oh. Sean now, is it?

CRYSTAL And he'd be all tanned and mysterious and brooding.

EDDIE And old.

CRYSTAL And he'd reach over and click the telly off. And then he'd stroll round the room, looking at me. Just looking at me. Looking at me all over. Undressing me mentally.

EDDIE Doesn't sound as if he'd need much imagination.

CRYSTAL And then he'd make his move, and I'd be engulfed by his big powerful arms. And we'd kiss. And oh boy, does he know to kiss. And I can smell him. Oh yes, he smells of, of pure Sean Connery. And then he'd lean back, and he'd rip off my flimsy see-thru nightie as easy, as easy as, pulling a curtain.

EDDIE Oh, lovely image.

CRYSTAL And then he'd start to unbutton his shirt, and as he did that, I'd kneel down, and I'd undo his belt, and I'd gently begin to ease off, oh yes, and then underneath –

EDDIE	Alright, alright, spare me the details.

(CRYSTAL *is getting into this more and more.*)

CRYSTAL	Right, so he's naked. And I'm naked. Apart from my stockings. I've still got those on. And I want him. I want him like nothing else, and then he takes me. Oh God, he takes me. Like some sort of silent deadly panther. And we do it. We do it. Every way possible. We even invent a few positions. And it just goes on. On and on all night. For hours and hours, and he doesn't say anything, just every now and then he mumbles my name, and I think I didn't know it was possible to feel all this, to feel this close to someone, to know somebody so intimately.
EDDIE	You didn't call him Sir Sean, then?
CRYSTAL	And then just as the sun is beginning to rise, and the first few rays of the virgin day are filtering into our temple of love, we reach, simultaneously, the most glorious and earth-shattering orgasm. Comparable only to a volcano. And we both collapse, like marathon runners crossing the tape, and he holds me, and he whispers my name, and I fall asleep. And I have a beautiful dream, and then, when I wake up, and he's gone. But it doesn't matter because I am happy, and I am fulfilled, and I know that I am the most special woman in the world.

(*Silence.*)

EDDIE	What is Sean Connery going to be doing in your bedroom? He lives in Barbados.
CRYSTAL	It's a fantasy. It doesn't matter where he lives.

(*Beat.*)

CRYSTAL	Eddie?

EDDIE	What?
CRYSTAL	Why don't you be Sean Connery?
EDDIE	Me?
CRYSTAL	Go on. Be Sean Connery.
EDDIE	Who are you going to be?
CRYSTAL	I'm going to be me. It's my fantasy.
EDDIE	I can't do a Scottish accent.
CRYSTAL	That doesn't matter. Just mumble.
EDDIE	Mumble?
CRYSTAL	Yes.

(CRYSTAL *gives an illustration of mumbling as Sean Connery.*)

EDDIE	I'm not doing that. That's bordering on the lunatic.
CRYSTAL	Oh come on, Eddie. Please. Go on. You'll enjoy it.

(EDDIE, *under pressure, gets up.*)

CRYSTAL	Why don't you go outside, Sean?

(EDDIE *tries to mumble.*)

CRYSTAL	And I'll get myself ready. Sean.

(EDDIE *mumbles again.*)

CRYSTAL	Oh yes, that's it. Sean.

(EDDIE *starts to act the part with a bit more confidence.*)

CRYSTAL Where do you want me, Sean? Oh yes, tell me how you want me Sean?

EDDIE Look, do you have to call me Sean?

CRYSTAL Do you want me here on the bed, Sean?

(EDDIE *mumbles.*)

CRYSTAL I'm going to be here waiting for you, Sean. Why don't you go outside, Sean, and I'll get myself ready.

EDDIE Look, it's just the Sean bit –

CRYSTAL Eddie will you go outside. I mean Sean, Sean, OK, you're here now, just stroll around the room, Sean, that's it, that's it, I'm here waiting for you Sean, oh yes, Sean, that's it, stroll, and look at me, Sean, undress me mentally, Sean –

EDDIE Stop calling me Sean!

(*Silence.*)

CRYSTAL Are you going to play or not?

EDDIE I can't. It's not natural.

(*Silence.*)

EDDIE Why don't you read your book?

CRYSTAL I don't want to read my book now, thank you very much for asking.

(*Silence.*)

EDDIE What's the time?

(*Neither of them move. Fade to black.*)

Scene Six

A series of short scenes that reflect the passing of time.

CRYSTAL *is reading, but they are both very bored.*

EDDIE   What's the time?

                  (*Silence.*)

CRYSTAL   Time you got yourself a watch that works.

                  (*Snap to black.*)

EDDIE *comes out of the bathroom. His flies are undone.*
CRYSTAL *notices. Black-out.*

EDDIE *stands by the window.* CRYSTAL *has given up on her book.*

EDDIE   Still raining.

                  (*Silence.*)

EDDIE   The garden needs it though, as my –

CRYSTAL   My mum always says.

                  (*Silence.*)

EDDIE   Why don't you read your book?

CRYSTAL   I'm fed up with reading.

                  (*Silence.*)

EDDIE   I'm not surprised, all those pages.

                  (*Snap to black.*)

EDDIE *is experimenting with making faces with a pillow.*
CRYSTAL *turns to look at him. Snap to black.*

CRYSTAL *stands at the window.* EDDIE *sits on the bed.*

CRYSTAL	What a ghost town.

(EDDIE *starts to wander round the room.*)

CRYSTAL	Why does everyone in this town look ill or bored?

(*Silence.*)

CRYSTAL	They all look as though they've given up the will.

(EDDIE *is now looking in a drawer/bedside cabinet.*)

CRYSTAL As though they've said I'm not going to bother any more.

EDDIE Have you ever noticed how hotel furniture always has a funny smell?

CRYSTAL This is it. Life, the great non-starter.

EDDIE Hey look at this.

(CRYSTAL *turns to look at* EDDIE.)

EDDIE There's some Scrabble in here.

(*Snap to black.*)

Scene Seven

Lights up as the Scrabble board goes flying.

CRYSTAL It is a word.

EDDIE It isn't.

CRYSTAL It is. I use it all the time.

EDDIE	It's slang. You cannot use slang. It's in the rules.
CRYSTAL	It is not slang.
EDDIE	It is.
CRYSTAL	It's a proper word. You say, my elbow's giving me a bit of gip. A bit of gip.
EDDIE	And gip is slang.
CRYSTAL	It is not.
EDDIE	It is, it's like, doubrey.
CRYSTAL	Doubrey?
EDDIE	Yea, as in, 'ooh where's the doubrey?'
CRYSTAL	Doubrey isn't slang.
EDDIE	It is.
CRYSTAL	It isn't.
EDDIE	Look, doubrey is not the word in question.
CRYSTAL	Prove it's not slang. Go on prove it.
EDDIE	I can't, can I? We haven't got a dictionary.
CRYSTAL	No, we haven't got a dictionary, and if we haven't got a dictionary, you should give me the benefit of the doubt.
EDDIE	Gip is slang. End of conversation.
CRYSTAL	It is not.
EDDIE	It is.

(*A pause in the argument. It is not over though. Lots of body language.* EDDIE *goes into bathroom and starts making noises aimed at annoying* CRYSTAL. *She seethes, and goes over to door and slams it.* EDDIE *rushes out, and sees* CRYSTAL *standing there.*)

EDDIE What did you do that for?

CRYSTAL Felt like it.

EDDIE What sort of world would we be living in if everyone just went round doing what they felt like?

CRYSTAL You think I'm thick, don't you?

EDDIE Well I don't think you should choose slang as your specialist subject on 'Mastermind'.

CRYSTAL I know what slang is.

EDDIE Gip is slang. My neighbour used to have a dog called Gip. It was short for Gypsy, so it was both a name and an abbreviation.

CRYSTAL You don't half talk some rubbish sometimes.

EDDIE So it's disqualified on both counts.

(CRYSTAL *decides enough is enough, and starts packing her bag.*)

EDDIE What are you doing?

CRYSTAL None of your business.

EDDIE Alright then. Just go. See if I care.

CRYSTAL Where is my dental floss?

EDDIE I haven't touched your dental floss.

CRYSTAL — What a charming person you are. You cheat at Scrabble, and you steal women's dental floss.

EDDIE — I don't even know what dental floss is.

CRYSTAL — Excuse me.

(CRYSTAL *moves round the room getting something.*)

EDDIE — And how do you think you're going to get out of this place?

CRYSTAL — I'll thumb a lift.

EDDIE — In this weather? You'll be lucky.

CRYSTAL — Alright, I'll catch a train.

EDDIE — Catch a train? You don't even know where the station is.

CRYSTAL — Well maybe I will have to summon up all my deductive powers and ask someone.

EDDIE — And what happens if you ask some weirdo? Eh? Eh? Have you thought about that?

(CRYSTAL *is at the door.*)

CRYSTAL — Goodbye Eddie. Have a good life.

(*She turns to go.*)

EDDIE — Crystal . . .

(*She stops.*)

EDDIE — Let's toss for it.

(*Beat.*)

CRYSTAL — Toss for what?

EDDIE	Whether you leave or not. Heads you go, tails you stay.
	(CRYSTAL *is slightly taken aback, but then –*)
CRYSTAL	Heads I stay, tails I leave.
EDDIE	OK.
	(EDDIE *fetches out a coin, and tosses it.*)
EDDIE	Tails. That means you've got to stay.
CRYSTAL	No, no, we just said if it's tails, I leave.
EDDIE	We didn't.
CRYSTAL	We did.
EDDIE	You swapped it round.
CRYSTAL	Yes, to heads I stay, tails I leave.
	(*Beat.*)
EDDIE	Best out of three?
CRYSTAL	Heads I stay, tails I leave.
EDDIE	OK.
	(EDDIE *tosses the coin.*)
EDDIE	Heads.
	(EDDIE *tosses again.*)
EDDIE	Tails. You leave.
CRYSTAL	Bye bye, Eddie.
	(*Beat.*)
EDDIE	Don't go, Crystal.

CRYSTAL	Eddie, I've been here before, I don't like the scenery.
EDDIE	Don't go. Please.
CRYSTAL	Give me one good reason.
EDDIE	I'll change.
CRYSTAL	You'll change? What into?
	(*Beat.*)
EDDIE	Don't go. Look it's stopped raining. It's an omen.
CRYSTAL	It hasn't stopped raining.
EDDIE	It's only spitting.
	(CRYSTAL *shuts the door and comes back into the room. Silence.*)
EDDIE	What did you mean, you've been here before?
CRYSTAL	I've had hundreds of arguments like this.
EDDIE	Have you?
CRYSTAL	Yep.
EDDIE	Who with?
CRYSTAL	My husband.
	(*Beat.*)
EDDIE	Your husband? Your husband?! Where did he come from?
CRYSTAL	Lytham St Anne's, originally.
EDDIE	I, I take it this means you're married?

CRYSTAL	Was married, Eddie. Was married.
	(*Beat.*)
CRYSTAL	Nine years I was married. Two years engaged. I'd been going out with him a year before that. All together twelve years. Twelve years of convenient boredom and silent desperation.
EDDIE	You got any kids?
CRYSTAL	No.
EDDIE	What, did he walk out on you then?
CRYSTAL	No, Eddie, I walked out on him. I walked out on him. He didn't walk out on me. I walked out on him.
	(*Beat.*)
CRYSTAL	I remember thinking at my wedding that, oh it'll be alright in a minute because someone like Dustin Hoffman in that film was going to burst in and rescue me. But who was I kidding? And then I was saying 'I do' and smiling for the photos, and saying thank you for presents that I never wanted in the first place. We actually got given three toast racks. What did they think I was going to do? Start a bed and breakfast?
EDDIE	Oh yea, I remember he drags her out of that church and they get on the bus.
CRYSTAL	Who did I think was going to do that? I didn't know any Dustin Hoffmans. I'd been too busy plighting my troth to Steve the carpet-fitter and popping down to Pronuptia every weekend to meet any Hollywood film stars.
EDDIE	Good point.

CRYSTAL	So, got married. Woke up on my honeymoon with a screaming hangover and a man with an unnatural interest in felt. The next nine years passed in a blur of tedium and the ever-growing feeling that this wasn't what life was supposed to be, and then, one night, he was asleep on the sofa, and I watched this programme about this woman who had travelled across the Sahara on a bicycle, and I knew there and then that I had to leave. So, the very next morning I wrote him a note, got the bus into town, found a flat above a dry-cleaners, and got my haircut.

(*Beat.*)

CRYSTAL	And changed my name as well.
EDDIE	Eh?
CRYSTAL	Crystal's not my proper name.
EDDIE	What is?
CRYSTAL	Babs. Barbara. But always Babs. Babs Bennett. That's me.
EDDIE	You changed it? Just like that.
CRYSTAL	Yep.
EDDIE	You didn't have to ask anyone's permission?
CRYSTAL	No. I just started calling myself Crystal. I wanted a name with a bit of sparkle.
EDDIE	But really you're still called Babs?
CRYSTAL	Technically, yea. I suppose I am.
EDDIE	You mean to say, you just created a new you?
CRYSTAL	I suppose I did. But then I'm not sure if I've created the right person. Do you ever get that

	feeling in the middle of the night, and you can't sleep, and everything's racing through your head, and you think, how did I get here, who the hell am I?
EDDIE	No. I'm a very sound sleeper, me.
	(*Beat.*)
EDDIE	Twelve years eh?! I'll tell you though, that's a drop in the ocean compared to some. My Mum's best friend, she's just had her Golden Wedding Anniversary. Just think, that could have been you.
CRYSTAL	Eddie, that is the point.
EDDIE	What point?
CRYSTAL	The point. That is the point above all other points. I could have been married for fifty years.
EDDIE	You get a telegram from the Queen.
CRYSTAL	No you don't.
EDDIE	No you don't. I don't know why I said that.
	(*Beat.*)
CRYSTAL	What's the longest you've been with anyone, Eddie?
EDDIE	Who me?
CRYSTAL	No the other bloke over there called Eddie with the lamp shade on his head.
EDDIE	Oh right, er, let's see, I don't think I've ever, you know, sat down and, blimey the longest, do you want it exact?
CRYSTAL	Approximately. I don't mind.

EDDIE	Six weeks.
CRYSTAL	Six weeks?
EDDIE	Seven maybe. Depends if you count it from the first time I bought her a drink.
CRYSTAL	What did she do?
EDDIE	She worked in the music business.
CRYSTAL	Really. Doing what?
EDDIE	(*feebly*) She used to work in 'Our Price' part-time.

(*Beat.*)

CRYSTAL	Did she hurt you?
EDDIE	Nah. That's the way it goes.
CRYSTAL	What was her name?
EDDIE	Colette.
CRYSTAL	Nice name.
EDDIE	She was alright. Her dress sense was a bit, unusual. To be honest, I think she just liked me for my money.

(*Beat.*)

EDDIE	She was quite a free spirit actually. She used to drink pints of Guinness, and talk about doing this and that. And then we were supposed to be going to see this film one night and she didn't turn up and the next thing I heard she'd moved to Hebden Bridge.

(*Beat.*)

EDDIE	She did write me a letter. She had an unusual turn of phrase. She said kissing me was a bit like kissing Sid James.

(*Beat.*)

EDDIE	I think she thought it was funny. I mean, I've always liked Sid James, but, I wouldn't want to kiss him.

(*Beat.*)

CRYSTAL	And I don't suppose she was too keen on you still living with your Mother?
EDDIE	Eh? Why do you say that?
CRYSTAL	Because you do, don't you?
EDDIE	No I don't.

(*Beat.*)

EDDIE	Just because I live with my Mum doesn't make me any less of a man or anything. She needs me. She suffers from very bad headaches. They come out of nowhere. Terrible they are. I'm going to be getting me own place very soon. I'm saving up. But I can do anything I want you know. I'm my own man, me. My room is sacrosanct. I've laid out a lot of money on it. I've just had some very snazzy lighting put in . . .

(EDDIE *runs out of conviction.*)

CRYSTAL	Eddie?
EDDIE	What?
CRYSTAL	Will you hold me?
EDDIE	Eh?

CRYSTAL	Hold me.
EDDIE	Hold you?
CRYSTAL	Yea. Just hold me.
EDDIE	What for?
CRYSTAL	Because I want you to.
EDDIE	Oh. OK.

(EDDIE *awkwardly holds* CRYSTAL.)

EDDIE	How's that?
CRYSTAL	Maybe, just a bit tighter.

(*Beat.*)

CRYSTAL	A bit less.
EDDIE	OK. I've got it.
CRYSTAL	That's fine, Eddie. That's . . . fine.

(*Silence.*)

EDDIE	Do you want to stay like this for long?
CRYSTAL	I'm thinking of staying like this forever.
EDDIE	Forever? Forever's a long time.
CRYSTAL	Forever's a state of mind, Eddie.
EDDIE	Is it?

(*Beat.*)

EDDIE	Hey I've just thought. Sid and Babs. That's us. Sid and Babs.

(*Lights fade.*)

ACT TWO

Scene One

EDDIE *and* CRYSTAL *are still in the same position, holding each other. Stillness.*

EDDIE	Can I let go now?
CRYSTAL	OK Eddie.
	(*They separate. A quiet, relaxed atmosphere.*)
CRYSTAL	I think I might have a bath. Do you want to scrub my back?
EDDIE	I'll get my flannel.
	(*Beat.*)
EDDIE	Hey, I've just remembered.
CRYSTAL	What?
EDDIE	That champagne never arrived.
CRYSTAL	Oh no, Eddie. We don't need champagne.
EDDIE	Yes we do. This is a celebration.
CRYSTAL	What of?
EDDIE	Us.
	(EDDIE *moves to the phone.*)
CRYSTAL	We don't need champagne, Eddie.
EDDIE	Oh, go on, shut up, of course we do.
	(EDDIE *phones room service. Throughout this speech* CRYSTAL *begins to become reflective. The easiness of previous disappears.*)

EDDIE　　Hello, is that room ser, oh hello mate, how are you? How's life in the fast lane? See. See what did I say? Thank you. Fantastic. So, very pleased things are looking up mate, but could I just, oh well that is the mysterious world of women for you, mate. So, do you think, fantastic mate, just pleased to have played a little part in your happiness, yes, and actually there is something you could do for me. Champagne. Bottle of. Like the one that never arrived last night. No. I'm sure mate. I can recognise a bottle of champagne when I see one, and I did not see one last night. I know mate, I know, you had other things on your mind, but you can make amends by getting me one double-pronto and all will be forgiven. If you insist mate, very generous of you. Yes, we must have a drink sometime, but not now mate, because I happen to be a bit busy. Yes, that sort of busy. Yes, one bottle of your very best house champagne. Two glasses. Nicely chilled. Yes, yes, for my lady friend and me. (*They share a joke.*) OK mate, over and out, bottle of champagne, and I'll be eternally grateful. Indeed. No, I'm sorted there mate, just the champagne. OK. Honestly, it was nothing. Look, I have to go, mate. I'm just happy for you mate, and I'll be even happier when that champagne arrives. That's the one. Room thirteen. OK. Smashing, What? The tipex was in the drawer. It always is. OK, must dash. My pleasure, mate. Cheerio mate. And you. Cheers. OK. Bye then. Bye mate. Yes, champagne. Yea, yea, good joke, mate. Alright. Bye. Bye, mate.

(EDDIE *gets the phone down.* CRYSTAL *sits on the end of the bed, heavy in thought.*)

EDDIE　　Champagne, on its way. All sorted.

(*Beat.*)

EDDIE　　You alright?

CRYSTAL	Yea, yea, I'm fine.
EDDIE	You've gone quiet.
CRYSTAL	Just thinking.
EDDIE	What about?
	(*Beat.*)
EDDIE	Crystal?
CRYSTAL	What?
EDDIE	What you thinking about?
CRYSTAL	I'm not sure. Things.
	(*Beat.*)
EDDIE	Hey what shall I call you now? I mean, if your real name is Babs, but I've been calling you Crystal, so, I mean, if you want me to.
CRYSTAL	Whatever you want Eddie.
EDDIE	OK, Crystal it is then.
	(CRYSTAL *makes a decision.*)
CRYSTAL	Let's go out.
EDDIE	What? Now?
CRYSTAL	Oh yea, get out of this flipping room.
EDDIE	Go for something to eat?
CRYSTAL	Chips. Fish and chips. And then we'll hit the arcades, and we can have some candy floss.
EDDIE	What about the champagne?
CRYSTAL	We'll have it with the chips.

EDDIE	Yea. Right.
CRYSTAL	Let's just do something.
EDDIE	I'm into that, yea.
CRYSTAL	Let's just go a bit stupid. Eh? Let our hair down.
EDDIE	Alright, alright, hey, we could go for a paddle.
CRYSTAL	Now you're talking. Let's go a bit crazy.
EDDIE	Yea, crazy, right, I'm into that.
CRYSTAL	Actually, let's go really crazy.
EDDIE	Really crazy.
CRYSTAL	Yea, let's get mad.
EDDIE	OK, yea, I'm up for it. Mad, yea. And crazy.
CRYSTAL	Let's get mad, let's get really mad, and do something outrageous.
EDDIE	Yea, let's get really really mad, yea, and just, do something
CRYSTAL	Why don't you dress up as a woman?
EDDIE	Hey, us two we're mad for it, aren't we?
CRYSTAL	And I'll dress up as a man.
EDDIE	Yea, mad and crazy, that's us . . . hold on.
CRYSTAL	That'll turn a few heads.
EDDIE	Hold on, hold on.
CRYSTAL	We could go into one of those wine bars near the pier.

EDDIE   Oi.

(*Beat.*)

EDDIE   Dress up as a woman?

CRYSTAL   Yea, let's get insane.

EDDIE   I'm not dressing up as a woman. What about my tash?

CRYSTAL   Shave it off. It's only a moustache.

EDDIE   Only . . . only a moustache?

(CRYSTAL *starts to chant 'shave it off, shave it off'.*)

EDDIE   Why don't you dress up as a woman?

CRYSTAL   I do it all the time.

EDDIE   Are you serious?

CRYSTAL   Oh, it's just a laugh. Have a bit of fun. Here, try this on.

EDDIE   Crystal! Crystal!? Hey, stop this. Stop it. Look, I am not dressing up as a woman, and I am definitely not, n-o-t, not shaving my moustache off for anyone!

(EDDIE *throws the proffered piece of clothing back across the room. A definite change in atmosphere.*)

CRYSTAL   So, what would you like to do, Eddie?

EDDIE   Well, I, I did happen to notice a local amateur group were doing a Gilbert and Sullivan.

CRYSTAL   Gilbert and Sullivan?

EDDIE	*The Pirates of Penzance.*
CRYSTAL	I sincerely hope you're joking, Eddie.
EDDIE	I'll have you know opera is very fashionable these days. It's a lot more accessible thanks to Pavarotti and those other two fellars . . .
CRYSTAL	Eddie!
EDDIE	What?
CRYSTAL	Wake up! Wake up!! Why don't you wake up!? You're asleep. You're . . . you're a blank space, you're a zombie, like, like everyone else in this town.

(CRYSTAL *goes to the window and starts to harangue.*)

CRYSTAL	Wake up! Come on, all of you, wake up! You have nothing to lose but your armchairs. Hey you. You in that ridiculous red hat. Wake up! Yes you. Don't look away. Hey here's a thought, live a bit. Do something.
EDDIE	Crystal!
CRYSTAL	Anything. Just do . . . anything. Something that says I am a free woman, I am not a bored couch potato who can't be bothered, just, hey and you can burn that shopping trolley for a start, it's a disgrace, you want to do something lady, here's an idea – just run into bloody Kwiksave and strip all your clothes off, and roll around in the fruit and veg section singing 'here we go, here we go, I've got lovely bunch of kumquats'.
EDDIE	Crystal, I think that's enough.
CRYSTAL	OK, I'll do it.
EDDIE	Crystal, no, no, look, you won't find a Kwiksave open this time of night.

CRYSTAL	Well, I'll find an Indian corner shop somewhere. I don't care, I'm crazy, me. Look at me, I'm a right crazy one, me. Get off.
EDDIE	Oi, stop it, will you just, Crystal!
	(CRYSTAL *starts to take her clothes off.* EDDIE *physically restrains her.* CRYSTAL *is shocked by the strength of* EDDIE'S *intervention. Silence.*)
CRYSTAL	That hurt, Eddie.
EDDIE	I'm sorry. Sorry. Sorry.
	(*Beat.*)
CRYSTAL	(*under breath*) Sid James.
EDDIE	What was that?
CRYSTAL	What?
EDDIE	You just said something.
CRYSTAL	Did I? No, it couldn't have been me. I'm dead quiet me. No, you must have the wrong person.
	(*Tension.*)
CRYSTAL	Sid James.
	(*Beat.*)
EDDIE	Babs.
CRYSTAL	Sid James.
EDDIE	Babs!
CRYSTAL	Sid James!
EDDIE	Babs!!

CRYSTAL	Sid James!!
EDDIE	Babs!!
CRYSTAL	I'm amazed you even got round to kissing her.
EDDIE	Babs? No wonder you changed your name.
CRYSTAL	Where did you snog her Eddie, in the back of your dynamite orange love machine was it?
EDDIE	Babs? Sounds like a really downmarket barmaid.
CRYSTAL	With your pongy aftershave and extra tongue action?
EDDIE	Yea, Babs, Babs the cheeky barmaid with the big tits, the big tits and the IQ of an underachieving bimbo.
CRYSTAL	And, oh how could we forget it, the tash from hell!
EDDIE	Only trouble, of course, is you haven't got big tits.
CRYSTAL	Who wears a tash like yours these days? Shall I tell you? Eh? Shall I tell you?
EDDIE	Yea, I'm all ears, lay it on me, Babs.
CRYSTAL	Sad people. That's who, really really sad people.
EDDIE	Oh God, you really think you're it don't you, Crystal the croupier, thinks she's so glam and sooo exciting.
CRYSTAL	It's a lot more interesting than what you do, mate.
EDDIE	Is it?

CRYSTAL	Flogging paper clips? What sort of a job is that?
EDDIE	Flogging . . . ? You, you couldn't begin to understand the, the demands and skill necessary for my job.
CRYSTAL	Remote control filing cabinets?! Am I missing something, or is that not the most stupid idea ever . . .
EDDIE	Oh right, standing behind that wheel all night, smiling at all those dirty old men breathing all over you, that's a proper job, is it?
CRYSTAL	Exactly. Dirty old men.
EDDIE	Looking you up down. Undressing you mentally.
CRYSTAL	It takes one to know one.
EDDIE	I am not a dirty old man.
CRYSTAL	Oh come on, you're all the same. Men, all you want is somewhere to stick it.
EDDIE	Well, I wasn't the one who brought the condoms, was I?
CRYSTAL	Yea, and why's that, real women, are they a bit of surprise, are they Eddie? Not like the ones in all the magazines, are we?
EDDIE	What are you going on about?
CRYSTAL	I bet you've got quite a collection.
EDDIE	You do not know what you are talking about!
CRYSTAL	Under your bed, in the wardrobe . . .

EDDIE	Hey, I'll have you know I am one of the most highly respected sales executives in the north of England.
CRYSTAL	Oh God, I bet you do a lot of that. Wanking. In your bedroom.
EDDIE	I've got certificates.
CRYSTAL	Oh yea, what for?

(CRYSTAL *illustrates what she thinks this might be for.*)

EDDIE	Sales executive of the year 1998, thank you very much.
CRYSTAL	Oh yes, Eddie's bedroom. Imagine it, with its snazzy lighting.
EDDIE	What's your flat like then? Eh? Have you got all mod cons, have you?
CRYSTAL	Oh yes, picture it, Eddie in his room of an evening.
EDDIE	I, I bet you haven't even got a decent telly. Some second-hand thing you can't even get a decent picture on.
CRYSTAL	Sitting there with his trousers round his ankles.
EDDIE	OK, you can stop this now.
CRYSTAL	But he's doing it ever so quietly because his Mum's downstairs.
EDDIE	That is not necessary.
CRYSTAL	I would love to see that, Eddie, caught mid-tug, your Mum's just popped up to say dinner's ready, and there's her little boy, his magazines spread out all around him –

EDDIE	Leave my Mother out of this!
CRYSTAL	Why have you never left home, Eddie? Scared of the real world, are you?
EDDIE	I'm not scared of anything, me. I did a sponsored parachute last year.
CRYSTAL	(*chants*) Scaredy-cat! Scaredy-cat!
EDDIE	Shut up!
CRYSTAL	Scaredy-cat! Eddie's just a scaredy-cat!!
EDDIE	Shut your gob, you cow.
CRYSTAL	Come on Eddie. Wake up! Wake up!

(CRYSTAL *starts to hit* EDDIE *with a pillow. He tries to take it at first. It just goes on, and eventually he has to react, and he grabs it.*)

EDDIE	Fuck off!

(*Silence.*)

CRYSTAL	Don't swear at me.
EDDIE	If I fucking want to I'll fucking swear at you as much as I fucking feel like.
CRYSTAL	Child.
EDDIE	Bollocks. Shit. Piss. Fuck me, I'm swearing. You're fucking not, are you? I fucking well am.
CRYSTAL	Grow up.
EDDIE	What, grow up and get married like you did?
CRYSTAL	At least I managed to sustain a relationship with someone longer than six weeks.

EDDIE	Yea, twelve years longer. Twelve wasted, empty brain-dead years. Well done Babs, I'm really fucking jealous!

(CRYSTAL *suddenly bursts into tears, with some force and hysteria.* EDDIE *is taken aback and is at a loss as to what to do. He desperately tries to calm her, but keeping his distance.*)

EDDIE	Hey Crystal, let's cool it . . . OK . . . cool . . . chill . . . Crystal . . . let's just take a step back . . . OK, hey look, I'm cool . . . take five, take five . . . that's it . . . no more shouting . . .

(CRYSTAL'S *sobbing eventually dies away. Silence. She then turns to* EDDIE.)

CRYSTAL	Shall we go out then?
EDDIE	Eh?
CRYSTAL	Go out. Shall we go out?
EDDIE	Er . . .
CRYSTAL	Get out of our brains.
EDDIE	Yea, ok, yea, let's go out and –
CRYSTAL	Have a really good time.
EDDIE	Yea, I'm up for that.
CRYSTAL	Let's get off our faces.
EDDIE	Right, now you're talking my language. Yea, yea, let's paint the town red!
CRYSTAL	Get completely shit-faced.
EDDIE	Right, yea, let's go sink a few.
CRYSTAL	I'll just wash my face.

(CRYSTAL *goes into the bathroom. Things have now become manic.*)

EDDIE Yea, let's go. Let's get out there, and par-tee! Oh yes, let's go, go, go, go. Go be wild. Let us go forth and sup huge amounts of alcohol, Crystal. I can't wait. Hey Crystal . . . Crystal?

CRYSTAL What?

EDDIE Do you know what, Crystal?

CRYSTAL What?

EDDIE We are lining ourselves up for one hell of a good time. Oh yes, we are party animals, Crystal. We are going to go out there and hunt ourselves down a good time. We are going to have the bestest good time known to man.

CRYSTAL What about woman?

EDDIE Man or woman, Crystal. I'm not sexist me, good times can equally be had by man or woman. Oh yes. Man and woman in best time ever shock. That'll be us, Crystal. That's me and you once we get out that door. How are you doing?

CRYSTAL Won't be long.

EDDIE Oh yea, let's go. Go. On the town. Me and you. Woo!

(CRYSTAL *enters from bathroom.*)

CRYSTAL How do you think I look?

EDDIE You look great!

CRYSTAL I'm ready.

EDDIE You look fantastic.

CRYSTAL Do you think?

EDDIE	You look beyond words, Crystal. Absolutely beyond words. What more can I say? Let's get out there and have ourselves one hell of a kickass good time baby!
	(EDDIE *is on his way out when* CRYSTAL *suddenly stops.*)
EDDIE	Crystal?
CRYSTAL	I don't like this jacket.
EDDIE	Crystal, you look fantastic. There is nothing wrong with that jacket.
CRYSTAL	I think I'll change it.
EDDIE	You don't need to change it.
CRYSTAL	I won't be a second.
EDDIE	Crystal, Crystal...
	(CRYSTAL *is trying on alternatives.*)
CRYSTAL	If I'm going to have a good time Eddie, I have to feel good about myself.
EDDIE	OK Crystal, you're right. Do you know what? You are right.
CRYSTAL	How does this look?
EDDIE	Oh my god, that is just, one hundred per cent better than the other one. That is, in my humble opinion Crystal, that is one jacket in search of a good time. Crystal?
CRYSTAL	It doesn't feel right.
	(CRYSTAL *goes back to trying clothes on.*)
EDDIE	What are you doing?

CRYSTAL	It didn't feel right, Eddie. Trust me.
EDDIE	Crystal, Crystal, I trust you, but, you looked brilliant. Sex on legs. Speaking purely as a man in the street, Crystal, you looked a million dollars.
CRYSTAL	It wasn't right. I'm very intuitive about these things.
EDDIE	Look, we'll go somewhere dark, nobody'll be able to see what you're wearing.
CRYSTAL	What about this one?
EDDIE	Fantastic. You'll knock 'em dead. Pow. Zap. Dead as a do-wotsit.
CRYSTAL	Oh, what about this one?
EDDIE	That one's great. Actually, I take back all I said about the other one because really, really Crystal, I meant that one.
CRYSTAL	You didn't like the other one?
EDDIE	No, no, not saying that, Crystal. Not saying that. Actually, now I think about it, they are both equally knock-out.
CRYSTAL	You're not just saying that?
EDDIE	No, I'm saying it because I mean it. Crystal, Crystal, what are you doing?
CRYSTAL	I can't make up my mind!
EDDIE	What is wrong with the one you're wearing?
CRYSTAL	There's no need for that tone, Eddie.
EDDIE	Crystal, please . . .

CRYSTAL	Maybe going out isn't such a good idea after all?
EDDIE	Crystal, that jacket you're wearing is the one. Believe me. That is the jacket, imagine that jacket out of this door, out on the town, out there Crystal, that jacket demands to be out there Crystal, it screams take me out, please take me out, I want to go out with Eddie and have a good time!

(*Beat.*)

CRYSTAL	Do you think?
EDDIE	Crystal, if that jacket was a filing cabinet, I could sell a truckload.

(*Beat.*)

CRYSTAL	What about my tights?
EDDIE	Perfect.
CRYSTAL	They haven't got a ladder in or anything?
EDDIE	No, they are unblemished Crystal. They are great, really, really great.
CRYSTAL	I wish I had an iron.
EDDIE	Hey, I wish I had a million pounds tax-free. Let's go.
CRYSTAL	Tell me the truth, is this OK?
EDDIE	It is out of this universe. Let's go!
CRYSTAL	Do you think?
EDDIE	Yes I think. Let's go! Let's go rock and roll.
CRYSTAL	OK. I'm ready.

EDDIE	Oh yes! The crowd goes wild. They are on the pitch, Crystal has said she is ready!
CRYSTAL	Are you being sarcastic, Eddie?
EDDIE	No, I'm just having a bit of fun, remember that, come on, let's go.
CRYSTAL	Shall we go?
EDDIE	No. Let's go.
CRYSTAL	Let's go and have some fun.
EDDIE	Fun, fun, fun!
CRYSTAL	Let's go.
EDDIE	Halle-bloody-juah we are going! Get out of the way for we are coming through. Oh yes. Oh yes siree, we have lift off.
	(CRYSTAL *has stopped.* EDDIE *realises this after a moment. He is beginning to get fed up with her behaviour.*)
EDDIE	What? What is it?
CRYSTAL	Your trousers, Eddie.
EDDIE	What about them?
CRYSTAL	Don't you think you should change them?
EDDIE	Come on, let's go.
CRYSTAL	You've had them on all weekend.
EDDIE	Well, I like them, don't I?
CRYSTAL	Go on Eddie, change them.
EDDIE	Is this a joke?

CRYSTAL	Change your trousers, Eddie. I don't want to go out with a man who doesn't change his trousers.
EDDIE	What?
CRYSTAL	All I'm asking you to do . . .
EDDIE	No.
CRYSTAL	Just change . . .
EDDIE	No. No, I am not changing my trousers.
CRYSTAL	That is typical, that is.
EDDIE	What is?
CRYSTAL	I spend all this time tarting myself up and you can't even be bothered to change your trousers.

(EDDIE *gives up and comes back into the room.*)

EDDIE	OK, OK, let's stay in. Like all the other zombies in this town.
CRYSTAL	There's no need to take that attitude.
EDDIE	We can watch the telly. Apparently there's a very interesting nature programme on BBC2.
CRYSTAL	I'm really not sure that I like you very much.
EDDIE	You can get your knitting out because I'll probably fall asleep on the sofa anyway.
CRYSTAL	In fact, I know I've never liked you very much.
EDDIE	Hey, maybe you could knit a nice colourful cardy for that Fred the weatherman. He's such a lovely little man, don't you think.

CRYSTAL	OK, I've had enough.
EDDIE	Well, why don't you piss off, then?

(*Beat.*)

CRYSTAL	Say please.

(*Beat.*)

CRYSTAL	Say please.

(*Beat.*)

EDDIE	Piss off.

(*They stare at each other.*)

EDDIE	Please.

(CRYSTAL *gets her stuff together, and exits.* EDDIE *is all bravado. He saunters to the door, and v-signs. He then realises she has actually gone. He sinks onto the bed.*)

Scene Two

A nightclub. EDDIE *enters. He is on the way to being drunk. He talks to a woman who we cannot see.*

EDDIE	Excuse me love, do you, do you mind if I park myself here for a bit? I'm on the karaoke in a minute. Yea, not bad. Apparently I have a lower register not dissimilar to Tom Jones. Register. Yea, just a joke. Just an attempt to oil the wheels of social intercourse so to speak. Hey, how rude, do you fancy a drink? Now I'm here eh? Yea, go on, push the boat out, have what you want. You what? Oh right, I thought you were just talking nonsense there for a minute. Excuse me, excuse me, yes, could I have a Voodoo Madness, mate. A cocktail in a bottle? Who'd have thought it eh? Eh mate, bung a

couple of extra umbrellas in there, yea, go on,
and a cherry, and eh, a fluorescent straw whilst
you're at it. The works. Fantastic. There we go.
Bottoms up. So, you, er, do you come here
often? Oh right, that's quite a bit then. No, no,
I'm a stranger to these parts myself. It's a long
story, I won't bore you with the details. I just
blew in. And, do you have a name? Petra?
Petra. Hey wasn't that the name of that dog on
. . . OK, OK, won't mention it again. I'm sure it
must get a touch tiresome. Could have been
worse though, you could have been called
Shep. Sorry. Sorry. Names though, eh, funny
business, names. Between me and you, this
woman I happened to come down here with,
she, she changed her name, from Babs, to, get
this, Crystal. Just like that. Eh? Oh didn't I
mention that before? Well it's all over now.
Water under the bridge of experience. History.
In the past. A new start. Yep, I'll drink to that,
a new start. Exactly. Cheers. I mean, who does
she think she is? I really put myself out this
weekend. Smashing room. Sea view.
Champagne on tap. Everything a woman could
desire, and what do I get in return? A load of
grief. Hey, hey, what am I doing? You don't
want to hear this. So, so, what do you, what's
your line of business, Petra? Oh right, sounds,
interesting. I'm in sales myself. Cutting edge of
the stationery world. Hey did I say, this
woman, Babs-stroke-Crystal, she was a
croupier. Yea, with the, thing, and oh boy did
she think that made her special. Don't make me
laugh. A croupier? Three inches of make-up, a
split skirt, and any Tom, Dick or Harry could do
that job. Women? What's going on up there? I
mean, do you understand women, Petra? Well,
of course, you are a woman, that makes a bit of
a difference. But I'll tell you this for nothing
Petra, do not get involved with a married
woman. Oh yes, you may very well look
horrified, yes, she was married. Just sprung it
on me. Out of the blue. Just like that. I'm a free
spirit, me. I don't want to be dealing with all

this, this, emotional baggage. Emotions? Who needs them? Eh? Where is she now? I do not know. And do you know what, Petra? I do not care. I do not give a monkey's. She has burnt her boat as far as I am concerned. You can spend too long moping about in this world. Move on, that's my motto. If she thinks I'm going to just stand about thinking about her, wondering what went wrong, she, she has got another thing coming, oh you off, are you? Oh right. OK. Yea, maybe I'll catch you later. OK. Hey you must have been thirsty. (*Petra is now obviously heading for the door.*) OK, you look after yourself, and eh if you happen to see a deranged looking woman wearing some (*Derisory comment, re:* CRYSTAL'S *jacket*), tell her from me that I am having an extremely good time. Yes, Eddie is having one hell of a good time. Tell her that. Oh yes, she is yesterday's news as far as I'm concerned. Bye Petra. OK, you tell her, she is nothing, you tell her that, she is out of sight . . . out of mind.

(*Petra has obviously left the bar.* EDDIE *deflates. He looks around. A man alone at a bar. The nod from the karaoke.*)

EDDIE   OK mate, coming now.

(EDDIE *exits. Music starts.*)

Scene Three

EDDIE *re-enters with microphone. He sings a maudlin, terrible love song of some sort. 'I Can't Live Without You' by Barry Manilow is a good choice. He reaches a low point.* CRYSTAL *enters, also with a microphone. She starts singing.* EDDIE *is over-joyed. They sing an excruciating duet. They move together, and say the following dialogue over the backing music.*

CRYSTAL   Eddie.

EDDIE	Crystal.
	(*Beat.*)
CRYSTAL	There aren't any trains until tomorrow.
EDDIE	Oh.
CRYSTAL	Then I tried to thumb a lift but only one car stopped, and that was a farmer just going down the road.
EDDIE	Oh.
	(*Beat.*)
EDDIE	Hey, Crystal . . .
CRYSTAL	That's my name.
EDDIE	Do you fancy a drink?
CRYSTAL	Oh Eddie, I thought you'd never ask.
	(*Snap to black. Drinking music.*)

Scene Four

Drinking music. A series of tableaus of EDDIE *and* CRYSTAL *on the town, getting bladdered.*

Scene Five

Lights come up on the pier. EDDIE *and* CRYSTAL *can be heard off-stage.*

CRYSTAL	Eddie, do you really think we should?
EDDIE	It's public property, isn't it?
CRYSTAL	Yes I know, but it's all locked up.

EDDIE	Look, we all pay our taxes, don't we? You pay your taxes, I pay a lot of bloody taxes. So if I want to take a stroll on the pier at three in the morning, no small-minded pen-pusher is going to get in my way.

(*Sound of wood breaking.*)

CRYSTAL	Ooh Eddie, aren't you strong?
EDDIE	Mr Universe, me! Oh yes, look at those biceps. He knows no danger.

(*Sound of more wood breaking.*)

EDDIE	Shit!
CRYSTAL	What have you done, Eddie?
EDDIE	I've got a buggering splinter.
CRYSTAL	Oh, let me kiss it better, diddykums.
EDDIE	Oh, that feels much better.

(*They suddenly burst on to the stage. Moonlight. They are pretending to play football.*)

EDDIE	Oh yes, he receives the ball in the middle of the park, and he's off, he sweeps past Viera, and the other one with the ponytail, and he does a little shimmy, and he goes through the defence like butter, Tony Adams, he falls over, and just he goalie to beat, and he smacks it, oh yes, the net's bulging, he's scored, it's the greatest goal ever scored, and it's pandemonium!

(CRYSTAL *is shouting any football cliché that comes into her head.*)

EDDIE	The crowd have gone bananas, oh yes, it's unbelievable, and they're all hugging me, all me

	mates, Becks, and Keano, and they're holding me aloft and –
	(EDDIE *falls over.*)
CRYSTAL	Over here son, on me head, on me head.
	(CRYSTAL *notices* EDDIE'S *absence.*)
EDDIE	I've fallen over.
CRYSTAL	Oh Eddie, what a great idea.
	(CRYSTAL *falls over.*)
CRYSTAL	I've fallen over, too.
EDDIE	I did it better.
CRYSTAL	No you didn't.
EDDIE	Yes I did.
	(*Repeat.*)
CRYSTAL	Oh, shut up.
	(*They contemplate the sky above.*)
CRYSTAL	I'm all dizzy.
EDDIE	Aren't stars beautiful?
CRYSTAL	What? All of them?
EDDIE	Yea, all of them. All sixty trillion billion million of them. Except that one over there, he's really ugly.
	(*Beat.*)
CRYSTAL	Do you think I'm beautiful, Eddie?

EDDIE	You are very beautiful, Crystal. And I mean that most sincerely.
CRYSTAL	Ooh you are awful, Eddie.
EDDIE	Yea but I'm right cuddly. Here, come over here.
CRYSTAL	No, you come over here.
EDDIE	No, you come over here.
CRYSTAL	I can't move, I'm too pissed.
EDDIE	Well, roll over here then.
CRYSTAL	No, you roll over here.
EDDIE	No, you roll over here.
CRYSTAL	No, you roll over here.
EDDIE	Hey, hey, I've got an idea.
CRYSTAL	What is it?
EDDIE	Let's roll at the same time.
CRYSTAL	That is a great idea. Let's roll.
EDDIE	Right. Roll.
	(*They both attempt to roll towards each other. They are both laughing hysterically, and generally having a good time. They miss each other by miles. They start crawling about, calling each others' name. They bang heads. More laughter.*)
EDDIE	Hey, I've got another idea.
CRYSTAL	Oh no, not another idea.
EDDIE	It involves me going away. But I shall return. Will you wait for me?

CRYSTAL	I'll wait for you Eddie.

(EDDIE *exits.*)

CRYSTAL	Eddie, what are you doing?
EDDIE	It's a surprise.
CRYSTAL	Hey Eddie, I've just remembered, we never got that champagne.
EDDIE	Phone room service.
CRYSTAL	Hey Eddie, that is a good idea. No Eddie, that is a very very good idea. Hello, is that room service? Oh hello mate, how are you? Oh did she? Did she mate? Oh that's terrible mate, yea yea women mate, yea, you want to use tipex mate, it kills all known germs.

(*Sound of a record being played at the wrong speed. It is 'Delilah' by Tom Jones.* EDDIE *comes back on, very pleased with his work.*)

EDDIE	What do you reckon, eh? I broke into the disc-jockey's little booth. He still plays records.
CRYSTAL	It's on the wrong speed.
EDDIE	Eh?
CRYSTAL	It's on the wrong speed.

(EDDIE *recognises what he's done.*)

EDDIE	Ah fuck it, it'll last longer. Hey, do you fancy a dance?
CRYSTAL	Oh yea, let's twist.
EDDIE	No, the funky chicken. Do do the funky chicken . . . Pogo.

CRYSTAL	Jive, Eddie, Eddie, jive.
	(*They proceed to drunkenly go through all of these dances. Room for quite a bit of ad-libbing. The jive degenerates and they fall into a kiss. It is a fairly long slobbery, grotesque moment. They look at each other.*)
EDDIE	Crystal. Oh Crystal.
CRYSTAL	Oh Eddie.
EDDIE	No, Crystal, can I be serious for a moment.
CRYSTAL	If you do it in a silly voice.
EDDIE	What?
CRYSTAL	(*silly voice*) Oh Crystal, you have beautiful eyes.
EDDIE	No Crystal, I just want to say –
CRYSTAL	Do it in a silly voice. Oh Crystal, you are very very beautiful.
EDDIE	No, look, Crystal, Crystal –
CRYSTAL	You have the mouth of Julia Roberts, and the bottom of Kylie!
EDDIE	Crystal, can I just say, you have made me very happy.
	(*Beat.*)
CRYSTAL	Have I?
EDDIE	You have, Crystal.
CRYSTAL	That's nice.

EDDIE
: I am so happy, Crystal. I am like a man in the, the desert of, of loneliness, Crystal, and you, you are my palm tree of happiness.

CRYSTAL
: Oh my God, he's gone all weird. Help, help, weird man alert.

EDDIE
: I feel we, you know, I think, Crystal, that we, we are two people, Crystal, and we, me and yourself, because, this moment, do you know what I'm saying?

CRYSTAL
: Not really.

EDDIE
: We are two people, who, and we are here, at this moment, we are standing right here Crystal, together, and this is us, we are here on this pier, and, we are here, and –

CRYSTAL
: Oh, shut up.

(They kiss again. EDDIE is even more ecstatic when he surfaces.)

EDDIE
: Oh, Crystal. I, I have touched something.

CRYSTAL
: Oh have you, Sid. You've touched something, have you?

EDDIE
: I have touched a higher plane. I'm up there, Crystal. I am up there. Look up there, that's me that is. I'm walking in the clouds, Crystal. I am at the summit of everything.

CRYSTAL
: Hey, hey, shall we go for a swim?

EDDIE
: I'd do anything for you, Crystal.

CRYSTAL
: Would you, Eddie?

EDDIE
: Anything. Name your price.

CRYSTAL
: Would you, would you dive off the pier for me Eddie, and swim down to the bottom of the

	ocean, and find me a beautiful pearl Eddie, would you do that?
EDDIE	I'd do that, Crystal.
CRYSTAL	Oh, you're just saying that.
EDDIE	No I'm not, I'll show you, I will show you.
CRYSTAL	You're cracked, you are.
EDDIE	I'd do that for you, Crystal. Here, stand back.
CRYSTAL	What are you doing?
EDDIE	I'm going to find Crystal whatever she wants.
CRYSTAL	Oh yes, Eddie's going for it.
EDDIE	I'm going to do it.
CRYSTAL	He's going to do it. Hey Eddie, this pearl, make sure it's half-decent, I don't want anything shoddy.
EDDIE	OK.
CRYSTAL	Hey Eddie, what are you doing?
EDDIE	I'm taking me trousers off.
CRYSTAL	What for?
EDDIE	I don't want them to get caught on the railings.
CRYSTAL	You are joking aren't you, Eddie? Eddie?
EDDIE	Oh yes, here we go. Hold those for me. OK. After three, one.
CRYSTAL	Eddie, this is a joke. Eddie, that's enough.
EDDIE	Two. Will you love me, Crystal?

CRYSTAL	Eddie, stop this. Eddie!
EDDIE	Three.
CRYSTAL	Eddie!!

(EDDIE *starts off.* CRYSTAL *screams. Black-out. 'Delilah' carries on, at the wrong speed. Loud.*)

Scene Six

Fade up on CRYSTAL. *She looks anxious. Eventually she crosses to another pool of light where* EDDIE *sits, dressing gown, pyjamas, and maybe some form of bandaging. He looks very sorry for himself. Silence.*

CRYSTAL	How are you feeling?

(EDDIE *mumbles something incomprehensible, but obviously extremely self-pitying.*)

CRYSTAL	Eh?

(EDDIE *mumbles again, slightly louder.*)

CRYSTAL	What was that?

(EDDIE *mumbles again, slightly louder.*)

CRYSTAL	I'm sorry Eddie, I can't understand a word . . .
EDDIE	I said, I'm feeling shit!

(*Silence.*)

CRYSTAL	They seem very pleasant. The nurses.

(*Silence.*)

CRYSTAL	The weather's lifting as well. Should be a nice day.

(*Beat.*)

CRYSTAL   You prat.

EDDIE   Eh?

CRYSTAL   You stupid, moronic half-brained tosspot, you –

EDDIE   Oi, oi, do you mind, I'm not well you know, OK, alright, thank you, thank you, yes I get the picture, alright!

CRYSTAL   You, you complete and total pillock. Never, ever, and I know we were drunk, and that, oh God you are so so stupid, I don't know if anyone's ever told you Eddie but you are possibly the most hopeless living human being ever –

EDDIE   Alright, alright, alright. Thanks a lot Miss Sympathetic for all your warmth and support. I could be six feet under now. Me and death shook hands.

CRYSTAL   Exactly.

EDDIE   I don't know why you're being so high and bleeding mighty, you're not entirely blameless are you?

CRYSTAL   But Eddie . . .

EDDIE   Oh yes, you played your part.

CRYSTAL   But Eddie, all things considered, at the end of the day, looking at it from every angle, I was not the one who actually went and bloody well jumped off the pier!

(*Silence.*)

EDDIE   I'm a survivor, me.

CRYSTAL   Are you?

EDDIE   Won't be able to keep me down for long.

CRYSTAL   No.

EDDIE   Listen to this. Doctor came in here earlier, and I said, 'Doctor, tell me the truth, after all this, am I going to be able to play the piano?' And he said 'I don't see why not' and so I said, I said –

CRYSTAL   'That's amazing because I couldn't when I came in here.'

            (*Beat.*)

EDDIE   Well, at least I was cracking jokes. Massive hangover, hairline fracture, and there I am, still cracking jokes. I'm a survivor, me. I'll always come bouncing back off the brick wall of life me. Oh yes, you just see. Bouncing back.

            (*Silence.*)

CRYSTAL   Nice flowers.

EDDIE   The bloke before left them behind.

CRYSTAL   That was considerate of him.

EDDIE   He didn't have much choice, he died yesterday afternoon.

CRYSTAL   Oh no.

EDDIE   The nurse was saying he was a smashing bloke.

CRYSTAL   Oh really –

EDDIE   And it was a complete freak accident. He was standing at this bus-stop and the sign fell off. Loose screw, they reckon.

CRYSTAL	Eddie, I, I don't really –
EDDIE	And apparently the council are denying all responsibility.
CRYSTAL	Eddie, will you have a bit of respect.

(*Beat.*)

EDDIE	Do you, do you fancy a cup of tea? They'll probably let me go down the canteen now.

(*Beat.*)

EDDIE	Crystal? Cup of tea and a wagon wheel? What do you say?
CRYSTAL	I'm off, Eddie.
EDDIE	Eh? You've only just got here.
CRYSTAL	No, I'm off.
EDDIE	Off?
CRYSTAL	Yes.
EDDIE	Off as in 'off'?
CRYSTAL	Yes.
EDDIE	Off as in 'fuck off out of my life altogether' off?
CRYSTAL	There's no need to get all bitter and twisted.
EDDIE	Bitter and twisted? Me? Bitter and twisted? Hey, I hope you have a really terrible life for saying that!

(*Beat.*)

CRYSTAL	My train's going in fifteen minutes. Goodbye, Eddie.

(CRYSTAL *begins to exit.*)

EDDIE I didn't mean that, Crystal.

(*She stops. She doesn't look back. She exits.*)

EDDIE Crystal? Crystal! Crystal.

(*Silence.* CRYSTAL *re-appears.*)

CRYSTAL I, I forgot to give you these.

(CRYSTAL *hands* EDDIE *a paper bag. She exits.* EDDIE, *crestfallen, takes out a bunch of grapes. He looks at them. He thinks. Music. He has an idea. He rises from the chair. The music also rises in volume. He begins to run. He is going for it. We see* CRYSTAL *at the train station, looking for details of her train. She is just moving off when* EDDIE *gets there.*)

EDDIE Crystal!

Scene Seven

The railway station. EDDIE *is out-of-breath. He still wears the dressing-gown and pyjamas.*

CRYSTAL Eddie . . . what . . . ?

(EDDIE *pants.*)

CRYSTAL What are you doing here?

EDDIE I, I ran all the way.

CRYSTAL What for?

EDDIE To see you.

CRYSTAL I, don't understand . . . my train, I'm just about to . . .

EDDIE	Crystal, I know we've had our differences, but –
CRYSTAL	It's going to leave, I, I can't –
EDDIE	I need to say something.
CRYSTAL	Eh?
	(EDDIE *takes a breath.*)
EDDIE	Shit, I've got a stitch.
	(EDDIE *slightly doubles over.*)
CRYSTAL	Eddie, I don't know what you want to say but honestly, I really do have to –
EDDIE	Crystal, Crystal, please, listen, I, I was thinking, back there, after you'd gone, I was thinking about us. Us. Me and you, Crystal, Eddie, Babs, Sid, and everything, and, and all that's happened, and, I was thinking, I was thinking, Crystal –
CRYSTAL	What? You were thinking what?
EDDIE	I was thinking how we're pretty similar me and you. We're both lost souls us, aren't we? We're both, I mean, neither of us know what we want, neither of us know what, oh God, I mean, we're both lonely, aren't we? That's the crux of the matter. We both need someone.
CRYSTAL	Eddie, I'm sorry but this is a bit . . . my train, I think –
EDDIE	Crystal.
CRYSTAL	What?
	(EDDIE *has taken out a small box.*)

EDDIE   Will you marry me?

               (*He opens the box to reveal a ring.*)

EDDIE   It used to be my Mum's. She, she said I could always use it if I met the right woman.

               (CRYSTAL *is speechless.*)

EDDIE   I know, I know this must be a bit of a shock. But, you know, we don't have to get married straightaway. We could do it in the spring. Eh? Think of that. What do you think? Oh, go on, Crystal, neither of us are getting any younger. I don't mean, I just think, you know, you get to a certain age, and, and I know you've been married before and all that, but this'll be different. Promise. Cross my heart. Crystal? And . . . it's not a bad time to get on the property ladder. Things have slowed down quite a bit. You know, and I've got quite a bit of money put away, you know, having lived with my Mum all these years . . .

CRYSTAL   Eddie.

               (*Silence.*)

EDDIE   So, what do you say?

CRYSTAL   My train, Eddie . . .

EDDIE   Crystal?

               (*Silence.*)

CRYSTAL   Oh Eddie, this is so . . . I, I can't believe that . . . how shall I put this? This weekend . . . I, I just thought . . . I am lonely, you're right . . . that's why . . . oh yes, this weekend has certainly been . . . an experience, oh yes, and, I think . . . your pyjamas are falling down.

EDDIE   Oh . . . right.

(EDDIE *re-adjusts his pyjamas.*)

EDDIE Is that a yes or a no?

CRYSTAL You are such a nice bloke, Eddie. I know that. It's . . . I bet there are hundreds of girls out there who would give their back teeth for a fellar like you. You've got a nice car, you're generous, you like a joke, you like saying good morning to anyone and everyone, but –

EDDIE What?

CRYSTAL You're not for me, Eddie. In a million years, you are not for me.

(*Beat.*)

CRYSTAL Oh, this is, this so mad. I mean, I'm not even sure that we should do this to each other, you know, men and women, that we should try and chain ourselves to each other till the end of time. I mean, imagine it Eddie, me and you, it's unthinkable, your clothes, your tash, your Mum. We'd last about a nanosecond.

(*Beat.*)

CRYSTAL Nothing personal.

(*Silence.*)

CRYSTAL Thank you though. I, I appreciate the, the, yea, thanks. I just think both of us could do better. And, Eddie, I mean that.

(*Silence.*)

CRYSTAL But now I really have to go.

(*Silence.*)

CRYSTAL I, I'm going to go.

(*Silence.*)

CRYSTAL Bye Eddie.

(*Silence.*)

CRYSTAL Bye.

(CRYSTAL *exits.* EDDIE *looks up, and watches her get on the train. He is obviously upset, but he thinks. A refrain of the karaoke music. He thinks, oh well, maybe she's right, and he straightens himself and he exits, trying to laugh at himself, and thinking tomorrow is indeed another day. One last look over his shoulder as the train pulls out. Music up. Lights fade.*)